All American Cooking

Savory recipes from savvy creative cooks across America

Created, Tested and Written by
Meryl Nelson

Researched, Helped and Encouraged by
Frances Thoman
(My Mom)
and
Bob Nelson
(My Husband)

Edited by
Shirley Sing
(My Super Friend)

BEFORE YOU BEGIN ...

The only appetizers you'll find in this book are those we've nicknamed Travel Teasers under the "State-istics". We hope these will whet your appetite for your own personal foray to our nation's historical, cultural, fun and scenic attractions.

The main purpose of the Teasers is to give information unique to each state, and since music, drama, art, and sports events occur in every state, and are necessarily seasonal, they were purposely omitted. However, all travel bureaus give up-to-date information on cultural and sports activities.

Since the actual 1990 population figures will not be available until 1992 -- we took the liberty of rounding the date as well as the figures, and gave you the best estimates we could locate.

NOW, ON TO COOKING ...

In preparing the book we started on the Eastern Seaboard with Colonial cooking, traveled westward, and have tried to give you an historical perspective as well as regional recipes.

We discovered that as settlers moved from place to place across America, they brought cooking experiences from both their diverse ethnic backgrounds and from the region they had left. When they blended this cookery with the food at hand in their new homes, dishes were born that are best described as All-American.

Our deepest thanks to the cooks and travelers who shared recipes and hints, and to the travel bureau personnel who responded to our request for updated information. And to ALL of you, whoever you are and wherever you're going, "Bon Appetit!"

Meryl Nelson
Shirley Sing
Frances Thoman

Published by
R&E PUBLISHERS
Post Office Box 2008
Saratoga, California 95070-2008
Phone (408) 866-6303
Fax (408) 866-0825

Fax, Phone and Written Orders Welcome

All American Cooking
Updated, revised second edition
Published October, 1991
Copyright 1991 by Meryl Nelson

10 9 8 7 6 5 4 3 2 1

ISBN 0-88247-902-4
LC No. 91-66552
Formerly published as "Cooking Coast to Coast"
Copyright 1984 by Meryl Nelson
This 'n That Press

Meryl Nelson's

Cooking Coast to Coast

Before You Begin..................ii	Nebraska (NE)....................60
Bonus Hints.......................4	Nevada (NV)......................62
Alabama (AL).....................6	New Hampshire (NH)..............64
Alaska (AK).......................8	New Jersey (NJ)..................66
Arizona (AZ).....................10	New Mexico (NM).................68
Arkansas (AR)...................12	New York (NY)....................70
California (CA)...................14	North Carolina (NC)...............72
Colorado (CO)...................16	North Dakota (ND)................74
Connecticut (CT).................18	Ohio (OH)........................76
Delaware (DE)...................20	Oklahoma (OK)...................78
District of Columbia (DC).........22	Oregon (OR).....................80
Florida (FL).....................24	Pennsylvania (PA)................82
Georgia (GA)....................26	Rhode Island (RI).................84
Hawaii (HI.)....................28	South Carolina (SC)...............86
Idaho (ID)......................30	South Dakota (SD)................88
Illinois (IL).....................32	Tennessee (TN)..................90
Indiana (IN)....................34	Texas (TX).......................92
Iowa (IA).......................36	Utah (UT).......................94
Kansas (KS)....................38	Vermont (VT)....................96
Kentucky (KY)...................40	Virginia (VA).....................98
Louisiana (LA)...................42	Washington (WA)................100
Maine (ME).....................44	West Virginia (WV)...............102
Maryland (MD)..................46	Wisconsin (WI)..................104
Massachusetts (MA).............48	Wyoming (WY)..................106
Michigan (MI)...................50	★ ★ ★
Minnesota (MN).................52	Breakfasts..................... 108
Mississippi (MS)................54	Lunches 112
Missouri (MO)...................56	Beverages 116
Montana (MT)..................58	Recipe Index..................117

POTPOURRI OF BONUS HINTS

One pint jar will hold a dry mix that, when mixed with water, is the equivalent of 9 (10½ oz.) cans of undiluted cream soup. Think of the room you'll save!

GWENN'S CREAM SOUP MIX

- 2 c instant non-fat dry milk
- ¾ c cornstarch
- ¼ c instant chicken bouillon
- 2 T dried onion flakes
- ½ t pepper
- 1 t thyme, optional
- 1 t basil, optional

Combine all ingredients. Mix well. Store in container with a tight lid. To make the equivalent of one can of soup, stir 1/3 cup of mix into 1/4 cup cold water; add to 1 cup boiling water in pan and stir over low heat until thick. If desired, add 1 tablespoon butter, chopped mushrooms, cooked celery or dried herbs.

For cream of tomato soup, replace water with tomato juice.

★Gwenn Koenig, Castalia, Iowa

Another interesting "make-ahead" is:

JERKY

- 2 lb. venison or round steak, ¾ inch thick
- ¼ t liquid smoke
- 2 T water
- salt and pepper

Cut meat into ¼ inch slices. (Partially freezing the meat makes slicing easier). Brush both sides of meat with liquid smoke mixed with water. Place strips in a glass baking dish and marinate overnight in a cool place (not the refrigerator).

Next morning remove meat, pat dry and place on oven racks so pieces touch, but do not overlap. Dry in 150° oven for 10 to 12 hours until completely dry. Store in air tight container. Great for snacks.

★ ★ ★

A few days before leaving, double recipes of casseroles, spaghetti, etc. Freeze extra portions in plastic pails with lids. You can use the pails later for special souvenirs — pretty shells, rocks, etc.

★ Pat Pepera, Manistee, MI

★ ★ ★

CAMPSITE POPCORN is fun! In the center of an 18 inch square of heavy aluminum foil place ¼ cup popcorn, 2 tablespoons oil, and ¼ teaspoon salt. Form foil into a bundle — leaving room for popping. Wire bundles to long sticks for cooking over campfires — shaking constantly until popping is done. Eat out of bundle, adding melted butter or grated cheese, if desired.

★ Mary Bjorkquist, Manistee, MI

Here's an ingenious sweet treat — PEPPERMINT ORANGE. Insert a peppermint stick candy into an orange and use as a straw.

FRESH BEAN SPROUTS

Grow your own fresh vegetables, by sprouting mung beans or alfalfa seeds. Soak 2 tablespoons of the former and 3 of the latter overnight in a quart jar. Next day, pour off water and cover top with nylon net or sterilize a square of nylon hose and secure with a rubber band. Turn the jar on its side and put in a warm, dark place. Rinse night and morning, draining each time, for 3 or 4 days. Use when alfalfa sprouts are about ½ inch long, beans about 1 to 1½. Excellent in salad, sandwices, stir-fry dishes. To "green" the alfalfa put in a sunny spot after sprouting.

★Carrie Fox, Downey, CA

★ ★ ★

If your RV unit has a power pack so electricity is available while you are driving, fix a chicken, roast or stew and put it in the crock-pot to cook as you travel. A towel in the bottom of the sink and towels packed around it will keep the pot in place.

★ ★ ★

FOIL BAKED VEGGIES save washing pots and pans. Cut tomatoes and zucchini into large chunks, onions, potatoes, carrots into smaller pieces. Put vegetables into "foil envelopes" made by folding 9 inch squares of aluminum foil in half. Crimp two sides. Insert "veggies"; dot with butter or margarine, sprinkle with salt and pepper. Seal open side. Cook on grill when barbecuing or bake in oven.

★ ★ ★

You may cook two foods at the same time if you include a double boiler in your camping utensils.

★ ★ ★

Keep an adequate supply of dehydrated foods such as onion, parsley, green peppers, etc. in case you run out of fresh.

★ Millicent Lane, Lansing, MI

★ ★ ★

Need an outdoor spot for washing hands? Slip a bar of soap down one leg of an old pair of panty hose. Tie the other leg to a branch near RV or tent. The soap is always handy and stays clean.

★ Becky Dinsen, Manistee, MI

★ ★ ★

Let the jiggling motion during traveling wash clothes. Place items to be laundered in a large plastic pail with a tight fitting lid. Add water and detergent.

★ Dorothy MacIntyre, Columbia Station, OR

ALABAMA — THE HEART OF DIXIE

Capital	Montgomery
Elevation	sea level to 2407 feet
Population (1980)	3,943,000
(1990)	4,052,000
22nd state	admitted Dec. 14, 1819
Tree	Southern Pine
Flower	Camellia
Bird	Yellowhammer

WHILE IN ALABAMA...

CAMP in a State Park — on a mountain-top, near a sparkling lake, or on the Gulf with its expanse of sugary white beaches.

FISH for a fighting tarpon in the Gulf Waters, or try your luck in a stream, lake or reservoir for bass, catfish and crappie.

SKI on the grass and play golf in the summer, then snow ski in winter at Alabama's one ski resort.

WANDER through 1,000 acres of azaleas and other blossoms at Bellingrath Gardens, or admire rhododendrons at De Soto State Park.

VISIT birthplaces — the Creek Indian Nation's at De Soto Caverns, W.C. Handy's log cabin, Helen Keller's "Little House at Ivy Green".

ADMIRE antebellum showplaces, historic forts, and a variety of museums including the George Washington Carver Museum in Tuskegee.

THRILL to the actual sights, sounds and "g" forces at the U.S. Space and Rocket Center in Huntsville.

LEARN about Alabama's heritage at the Alabama Music Hall of Fame, or the Civil Rights Memorial.

★ ★ ★ ★ ★ ★

WRITE for more information: Alabama Bureau of Tourism and Travel, P.O. Box 4309, Montgomery, AL 36103.

TRY

CRISPY FRIED FISH
with HUSH PUPPIES, *see Tennessee*
or
CHICKEN WITH SOUTHERN BARBECUE SAUCE
with boiled rice
or
SAUSAGED HOMINY, *see Indiana*
COLE SLAW, SOUTHERN STYLE
CORN ON THE COB *(grilled or boiled)*
WATERMELON OR OTHER FRESH MELON OR FRUIT

With over 25 varieties of both fresh and saltwater fish, and Alabama's open season for game fish year round, catching tonight's dinner should be easy.

CRISPY FRIED FISH

First cover fish with buttermilk, then sprinkle with 1 teaspoon salt per pound of fish. Let stand about ½ hour. Drain, then dip in flour and fry in hot fat about 1/8" deep over medium heat, about 5 minutes per side. Turn once and when both sides are golden brown, drain on paper towels.

HINT: Campers often cook a few strips of bacon until crisp, remove, and then cook the fish in bacon fat for extra flavor.

This typically southern sauce can be used with pork chops or short ribs, also. For one 2 to 3 pound chicken you'll need about ½ cup of sauce. Refrigerate any leftover sauce.

CHICKEN WITH SOUTHERN BARBECUE SAUCE

1 (2 to 3 lb.) fryer pieces, or 2 smaller chickens, quartered.

¾ c catsup	2 T vinegar
¼ c onion, finely chopped	1 T Worcestershire sauce
¼ c water	1 t seasoned salt
¼ c margarine or butter	1 T lemon juice
1 t dry mustard	Few drops of hot pepper sauce

Combine all ingredients in a small saucepan and simmer for 10 minutes over low heat.

Brown chicken pieces or quarters in large skillet. Add ¼ cup barbecue sauce (or more if needed to cover pieces). Put on lid, turn down heat and cook slowly for 20 to 30 minutes. Turn chicken with tongs (a fork pierces and lets juices escape); cover with more barbecue sauce and cook covered another 20 to 30 minutes until chicken is done. A little water may need to be added.

Add a Southern touch to cabbage salad by including Alabama-grown vegetables.

COLE SLAW, SOUTHERN STYLE

To your finely shredded cabbage, add some sliced or diced kohlrabi, cauliflower, or turnip. Toss with mayonnaise thinned with a bit of cream or milk. Saute a handful or two of coarsely chopped peanuts in a tablespoon of margarine and add at the last minute.

ALASKA — LAND OF THE MIDNIGHT SUN

Capital	Juneau
Elevation	Sea level to 20,320 ft.
Population (1980)	438,000
(1990)	534,000
49th state	admitted Jan. 3, 1959
Tree	Sitka Spruce
Flower	Forget-me-not
Bird	Willow Ptarmigan

WHILE IN ALASKA...

CAMP at Glacier Bay — Alaska's premier wilderness, and Denali, foot of Mt. McKinley; National Park; or choose State, County, City Parks everywhere.

CRUISE the Inside Passage fjords and take a "Flightseeing" plane that taxis right to your ship for a close look at the glaciers.

TRAVEL the Alaska Highway to Fairbanks. You can choose among about a dozen major and minor highways in Alaska, or use State-operated Ferryliners of the Marine Highway Systems in coastal areas where there are no roads.

GAZE at the huge fields of wildflowers; cranberry bogs; wild Dall Sheep, Caribou, Moose, Grizzly or Polar Bears; Sea Lions, Whales.

SEE Museums of Native Arts and Crafts, the celebrated Blanket Toss, Indian/Eskimo Olympics, Alaska Folk Festival, and the Alaska State Fair featuring 80 lb. cabbages and strawberries as big as apples.

VISIT the "Land of the Eskimo" above the Arctic Circle — realm of the Midnight Sun, Northern Lights, focal point of Eskimo Culture, and the Land of Totems in Southeast Alaska, home of the Tlingit and Haida Indians.

FISH your wildest dream in one of 3,000 rivers, 3 million lakes or a coastline longer than all of the lower 48's put together.

★ ★ ★ ★ ★ ★

WRITE for more information: Alaska Division of Tourism, Pouch E-400, Juneau, AK 99811.

TRY

MARINATED SALMON
or
DORIS' SURPRISE PACKAGE
or
BRAISED VENISON LOIN CHOPS, *see Idaho*
serve with
SUNSHINE SALAD, *see Montana*
CAMPFIRE POTATOES, *see Colorado*
VEGETABLE MEDLEY, *see Oregon*
DIPPIN' STRAWBERRIES

Alaskans bake, barbecue, broil, make souffles, salads and spreads out of their prolific salmon. A mother and daughter share two of their favorite "fixings".

MARINATED SALMON STEAKS

4 salmon steaks, 1" thick	3 T water
salt and pepper	5 T soy sauce
garlic powder	3 T lemon juice

Wet both cut sides of steak. Sprinkle lightly with salt, pepper and garlic powder. Mix water, soy sauce and lemon; pour over steaks and marinate at least one hour — preferably longer.

Grill over hot coals about 5-6 minutes per side or bake in a 400° oven about 20-25 minutes, until fish flakes easily.

★ Arlene Cross, Anchorage, AK

Arlene's daughter suggests:

EASY SALMON SPREAD

8 oz. cooked salmon	1 t lemon juice
(canned may be used)	T minced onion
8 oz. cream cheese	salt to taste

Remove bones and flake salmon. Mix all ingredients together and serve with crackers.

★ Sue Cross, Anchorage, AK

Outdoor cooking is almost a way of life in the summer. This recipe gives everyone a chance to add or subtract ingredients.

DORIS' SURPRISE PACKAGE

For each person:

1 serving size piece of round steak	1 thick slice zucchini
	1 clove garlic, halved
1 med. potato, halved lengthwise	½ tomato, peeled
	salt and pepper

Lay each steak on a piece of aluminum foil large enough to be folded, butcher style, over the top and to seal both ends. Add vegetables in the order given. Salt and pepper to taste. Grill for one hour over hot coals, or cook in a 350° oven for the same time.

★ Doris Carter, Plymouth, CA

In the summertime the most luscious strawberries come from Alaska's Matanuska Valley.

DIPPIN' STRAWBERRIES

Strawberries   Sour cream   Brown sugar

Wash strawberries, leaving stems on. Arrange in a large serving bowl. Put sour cream and brown sugar in separate small bowls. Each person dips a strawberry into the sour cream and then into brown sugar. Out of this world!

ARIZONA — THE GRAND CANYON STATE

Capital	Phoenix
Elevation	70 to 12,633 ft.
Population (1980)	2,860,000
(1990)	3,319,000
48th State	admitted Feb. 14, 1912
Tree	Palo Verde
Flower	Saguaro Cactus
Bird	Cactus Wren

WHILE IN ARIZONA ...

CAMP — in any of 96 State Parks, in Indian tribal campgrounds, or in two National Parks — Grand Canyon and Petrified Forest.

FIND — the site where Spanish conquistador Coronado first entered the U.S. in 1540, or visit Mission San Xavier Del Bac.

VISIT — prehistoric Indian ruins at Wupatki National Monument, the Havasupi Indian Reservation, Hopi Villages, or the cliff dwellings in Navajo National Monument.

STAND — by a dam site — Glen Canyon, Imperial, Hoover (highest in the world), discover London Bridge at Lake Havasu, explore Meteor and Sunset Craters.

WANDER — through Old Tucson and the nearby Arizona-Sonora Desert Museum. Admire Organ Pipe and Saguaro Cacti at their National Monuments.

ENTER — famed Oak Creek Canyon from the south at picture-postcard Sedona for full impact of its red rock formations and spires.

FISH — for trout below the dams, and in 500 miles of streams. Try your luck in the National Forest's fishing lakes, or in the Colorado River.

★ ★ ★ ★ ★ ★

WRITE — for more information: State Board of Tourism, 1100 W. Washington, Phoenix, AZ 85014.

TRY

ARROZ CON POLLO
or
PAN-BARBECUED SPARERIBS
or
CAMPFIRE STEAK, *see Oklahoma*
serve with
SHEEPHERDER'S POTATOES, *see Nevada*
COOL-DOWN SALAD
SHEER BLISS

You'll find reference to this recipe in Kansas, because early Kansan traders going into what is now New Mexico and Arizona introduced chili to Kansas cookery.

PAN BARBECUED SPARERIBS

3 lbs. country-style spareribs	1 T vinegar
1 med. onion, chopped	1 T chili powder
2 T brown sugar	¼ c catsup
1 t prepared mustard	1 c water

Brown spareribs in large skillet; drain off all but 2 tablespoons of fat. Stir in rest of ingredients. Roll spareribs in the sauce to coat well; cover and simmer until ribs are done. 4 to 6 servings.

Rice with chicken is a favorite combination in Mexican cookery. This version adds link sausages for a tasty touch.

ARROZ CON POLLO

1 (8 oz.) pkg. link sausages	½ c onion, chopped
1 (2½-3 lb.) fryer chicken	½ c celery, chopped
¼ c flour	1 (8 oz.) can tomatoes
1 t salt	1 (8½ oz.) peas, drained
1 T chili powder	1 c rice

Brown sausage in a large skillet. Remove, pour off fat except for 1 tablespoon. Shake chicken pieces in a paper bag with flour, salt and chili. Brown chicken pieces in sausage drippings. Add onion, celery and drained liquid from peas with enough water added to make 1¾ cups. Simmer about 30 minutes. Add rice, cut-up tomatoes and sausages. Cover and cook slowly until rice is done — about 20 minutes. Skim off fat; add peas and heat to simmering.

A nice change of pace to hot Mexican foods is:

COOL-DOWN SALAD

1 bunch (½ lb.) leaf lettuce	1 ripe avocado
1 can (10 oz.) mandarin oranges	¼ c sour cream
½ red onion, cut crosswise	¼ c mayonnaise

Wash and chill lettuce. Chill the mandarin segments.

Break bite-size pieces of chilled lettuce into a large bowl; add drained oranges. Cut onion into 1/8-inch slices and separate into rings. Add to the salad, with peeled, pitted and sliced avocado. Mix sour cream with mayonnaise; pour over salad and toss.

Our contributor names this deliciously simple dessert.

SHEER BLISS!

1 plain milk chocolate candy bar	Strawberries

Take a bite of chocolate, then a bite of washed strawberries.

★Ronda Wisniewski, S. Plainfield, NJ

ARKANSAS — LAND OF OPPORTUNITY

Capital	Little Rock
Elevation	55 to 1753 ft.
Population (1980)	2,291,000
(1990)	2,372,000
25th state	admitted June 15, 1836
Tree	Shortleaf Pine
Flower	Apple blossom
Bird	Mockingbird

WHILE IN ARKANSAS...

TRAVEL   the Great River Road, paralleling the Mississippi River and visit the many historic and recreation spots along the way.

SOAK   in the 47 mineral hot springs in Hot Springs National Park; then enjoy a spectacular view from the new 216-foot observation tower.

CAMP   in a State Park, including Crater of Diamonds, the only public diamond field in the U.S. You can keep what you find!

FISH   in numerous lakes and rivers. Greers Ferry Lake and nearby Little Red River provide trophy-size rainbow trout.

MARVEL   at the arts and crafts of the Ozark Mountain people at several parks which preserve their talents and life style.

ATTEND   an outdoor performance — from the Great Passion Play at Eureka Springs to the "Arkansaw Traveler" at Hardy.

ENJOY   an outdoor performance of the Great Passion Play at Eureka Springs, or enjoy the Delta Cultural Center, an $8.5 million project which preserves and interprets the Delta and its way of life.

* * * * * *

WRITE   for more information: Arkansas Dept. of Parks and Tourism, One Capitol Mall, Little Rock, AR 72201

TRY

TANGY PORK CHOPS with YAMS
or
HOT DOG GOULASH
or
CHILI-MAC, *see Utah*
serve with
HOT GREEN BEANS
FRESH FRUIT OR MELONS

This slightly sweet and spicy southern sauce can be used with chicken or spare-ribs, also. The recipe makes about 1½ cups of sauce. You'll need about ½ cup for four chops. Refrigerate the rest, but bring to room temperature before re-using.

TANGY PORK CHOPS with YAMS

4 pork chops	
1 c peach preserves	3 T lemon juice
¼ c minced onion	1 T prepared mustard
¼ c water	1/8 t cayenne pepper
¼ c margarine or butter	1 (16 oz.) can yams

Combine all ingredients except chops in a small saucepan, and cook over low heat for about 10 minutes. Keep at room temperature while browning chops in hot skillet. Pour over ¼ cup of sauce, turn down heat and let chops simmer until nearly done (about 20 minutes). Turn chops over, pour on another ¼ cup of sauce, then layer sliced, cooked yams over chops. Cover and simmer until yams are heated through.

Arkansas is a rice-producing state, and many regional recipes include this staple. The taco sauce reflects the Mexican influence of Southwestern Cookery on Arkansas' Texas boundary.

HOT DOG GOULASH

4-6 strips bacon, cut in one-inch pieces	2 c water
1 lg. onion, chopped	1 c regular rice
1 can (16 oz.) stewed tomatoes	1 t salt
	2 T taco sauce
	1 lb. wieners

Fry bacon in hot skillet. Remove bacon and drain off all but about two tablespoons fat. Saute onions until limp. Add tomatoes and water and bring to a boil. Slowly stir in rice. Add salt and taco sauce. Cover tightly and cook over moderate heat for 25 to 30 minutes. Stir in wieners, cut in 2-inch slices, and reserved bacon. Simmer until heated through.

HOT GREEN BEANS

Heat a can of beans until steaming. Drain the liquid, then add a dash of marjoram, or "devil" with a teaspoon of prepared mustard.

CALIFORNIA — THE GOLDEN STATE

Capital	Sacramento
Elevation	minus 282 ft. to 14,494 ft.
Population (1980)	24,724,000
(1990)	26,981,000
31st State	admitted Sept. 9, 1850
Tree	Redwood
Flower	Golden Poppy
Bird	Valley Quail

WHILE IN CALIFORNIA...

CAMP in any of 280 State Parks and Beaches some with wheel-chair-accessible campsites or in 6 National Parks — Yosemite, Lassen, Sequoia, Kings Canyon, Redwood and Channel Islands.

STAND in awe among the world's tallest trees — Sempervirens Sequoia on the north coast and Sequoia Gigantea of Yosemite and Sequoia Parks.

FOLLOW El Camino Real, route of Father Junipero Serra, and visit the 21 Missions he established from Southern to Northern California.

VISIT Badwater in Death Valley, lowest point in the U.S., and from there view 14,495 foot Mt. Whitney, highest in the lower 48.

INCLUDE the Mother Lode Gold Country on your way to Lake Tahoe. Backpack in the High Sierras with horses, mules, even llamas.

TOUR Olvera St., Movie Studios, La Brea Tar Pits, Forest Lawn, Theme Parks, Farmer's Market, World-Famous Beaches in the Los Angeles area.

RIDE the cable cars in San Francisco, then see Chinatown, Fisherman's Wharf Golden Gate Park, Ferry Building, U.S. Mint, Coit Tower.

★ ★ ★ ★ ★ ★ ★ ★

WRITE for more information: Office of Tourism, 801 K Street, Suite 1600, Sacramento, CA 95814.

TRY

CHOP SUEY BURGERS
or
TACO SALAD
or
KITCHEN STOVE CLAM BAKE, *see Oregon*
serve with
GREEN AND GOLD SALAD
STIR-FRY VEGETABLES, CHINESE STYLE
FRESH FRUIT OR MELONS

Chinese, called to California from their homeland to help build the first transcontinental railroad, added exotic new tastes to American cuisine, including the popular:

STIR-FRY VEGETABLES, CHINESE STYLE
(Chop Suey)

To VEGETABLE MEDLEY *(see Oregon)*, add water chestnuts, bamboo shoots, and soy sauce to taste. Dried Chinese mushrooms, soaked 15 minutes until soft and sliced into strips, give a true oriental flavor. All vegetables should be cut diagonally in rather large pieces. Add a cup or two of cooked chicken or pork — cut into strips, or shellfish, for a full meal.

For camping, we cut the vegetables into smaller pieces for:
CHOP SUEY BURGERS

1 lb. ground beef	2 T cornstarch
2 c chop suey*	8 hamburger buns, split,
2 T soy sauce	buttered and toasted
⅓ c water	1 (3 oz.) can crisp noodles

Brown beef, drain fat; add vegetables. Stir water and soy sauce into cornstarch; add to the hamburger mixture, stirring until thickened. Spoon onto bottom halves of buns. Crumble noodles over each sandwich; cover with top halves of buns.
*May use 1 (16 oz.) can chop suey vegetables

A current favorite of Californians — North and South is:
TACO SALAD

1 lb. ground beef	½ head shredded lettuce
1 (16 oz.) can chili beans	2-3 c corn chips
1 (8 oz.) can tomato sauce	1 c cheddar cheese,
1 T chili powder	shredded
½ t cumin	chopped onion, optional
1 t garlic salt	sour cream, optional

Brown beef until crumbly; drain off fat. Add beans, tomato sauce and seasonings. Cook 5 minutes. Put lettuce and coarsely crumbled corn chips in a large bowl. Mix well. Spread hot mixture over the lettuce and chips. Sprinkle with cheese; garnish with whole chips. Top with onion and a dollop of sour cream. 4 servings.

GREEN AND GOLD SALAD

Alternate overlapping avocado slices and orange segments in a ring on top of lettuce on individual salad plates. Mix equal quantities of sour cream and mayonnaise for dressing.

COLORADO — THE CENTENNIAL STATE

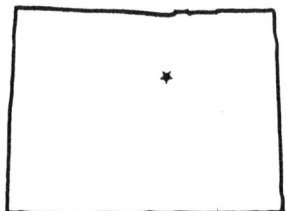

Capital	Denver
Elevation	3350 ft. to 14,433 ft.
Population (1980)	3,045,000
(1990)	3,267,000
38th State	admitted Aug. 1, 1876
Tree	Spruce
Flower	Columbine
Bird	Lark Bunting

WHILE IN COLORADO ...

CAMP in State and Federal Forests, Parks and Recreation areas as well as the Denver Mountan Park System.

VISIT Mesa Verde's mysterious Indian Ruins and Pino Nuche Pu Ra Sa to discover Indian culture — from 1000 years ago to modern times.

DARE to be adventuresome on one of two narrow-guage railroads, or walk across the world's highest suspension bridge at Royal Gorge.

TOUCH four states at the same time — the only place in the country where four meet at one point.

INCLUDE Red Rocks Amphitheatre with its amazing acoustics in your tour of Denver; and the Air Force Academy at Colorado Springs.

DRIVE to the summit of Pikes Peak or Mount Evans; but you must climb to reach the top of any of the 51 other 14,000 footers.

FISH for Rainbow, Brook, Brown, Cutthroat in any of 7000 miles of streams, 2850 lakes, 360 reservoirs. Ski world-famous Aspen and Vail.

★ ★ ★ ★ ★ ★

WRITE for more information: Colorado Tourism Board, 1625 Broadway, Suite 1700; Denver, CO 80202. 1-800-433-2656 or (303) 592-5410.

TRY

DENVER SANDWICH
or
WHOLE TROUT COOKED IN FOIL
(Eisenhower Style)
or
GRILLED LEMON CHICKEN
serve with
CAMPFIRE POTATOES
SLICED TOMATOES
CHERRY CRISP, *see Michigan*

This recipe was born in prairie schooner days, when eggs were hauled along hot, dusty trails for so long that their unpleasant strong flavor had to be disguised with a liberal amount of onions.

DENVER SANDWICH

½ lb. ground beef
or ½ lb. chopped ham
1 large onion, chopped
salt and pepper
4 eggs, slightly beaten
with 4 T water

Cook beef (or ham) and onion in a medium frypan until lightly browned. Drain off most of the fat. Stir in salt and pepper, then pour eggs over cooked meat. On low heat, scramble until eggs are set as you like. Serve over buttered toast or toasted English muffins.

President Eisenhower liked to cook some of the Colorado trout he caught this easy way.

WHOLE TROUT COOKED IN FOIL

Whole trout, about 1 lb.   salt and pepper   oil

For each serving, tear off a piece of heavy duty aluminum foil big enough to be folded over fish. Pour a little oil in the center of the foil, then place fish on foil, turning once to oil both sides. Sprinkle cavity of trout with salt and pepper.

Bring foil up over the trout, sealing edges with a double fold. Now double fold both ends. Place packets on grate over medium hot coals; cook about 15 minutes, turning 2 or 3 times.

To serve, transfer foil covered fish to plates. Open foil, turn back edges and crimp to stay. When fish is eaten from the foil container there are no fishy plates to wash.

Not lucky enough to catch a trout for the above recipe? You can continue the tradition of the Coloradan's delight for barbecuing with:

GRILLED LEMON CHICKEN

1 broiler-fryer   ¼ c butter or margarine   ¼ c lemon juice

Cut fryer into quarters, remove skin if desired. Melt butter and stir in lemon juice. Place chicken on a lightly greased grate above hot coals. Brush with marinade, and cook about 30 minutes, turning and brushing with marinade 3 or 4 times. 4 servings.

CAMPFIRE POTATOES

Potatoes, medium size   Oil   Aluminum foil

Scrub potatoes well; rub skins with oil. Wrap potatoes in two thicknesses of foil. Place directly on hot coals to bake. Turn every 10 minutes or so. (Or bury in the coals and you won't have to turn them.) Takes 45 - 60 minutes.

CONNECTICUT — THE CONSTITUTION STATE

Capital	Hartford
Elevation	sea level to 2380 ft.
Population (1980)	3,153,000
(1990)	3,189,000
5th State	admitted Jan. 9, 1788
Tree	Nutmeg
Flower	Mountain Laurel
Bird	Robin

WHILE IN CONNECTICUT...

CAMP   in State Parks, including Hammonasset Beach with its two-mile sandy shore, or Devil's Hopyard, featuring a river gorge and waterfalls.

VISIT   homesteads — Nathan Hale's, built by his father in 1776; Mark Twain's Victorian mansion; Harriet Beecher Stowe's "cottage".

RELIVE   whaling days at Mystic, a 19th century maritime village; sail on a schooner; cross the Connecticut River on a ferry; take an Oceanographic Cruise.

TOUR   Museums -- from P.T. Barnum to Noah Webster, Kerosene Lamps to Trolleys, American Indian Archeological to American Clock and Watch.

ADMIRE   the nation's oldest State House, classic colonial saltboxes with massive central chimneys, lavish 19th Century mansions.

WANDER   onto side roads to catch vibrant Fall color. Try us in Winter for ski sports and ice-skating, ice-fishing, ice-boating.

FORM   a group and harken back nostagically in a horse-drawn sleigh or, without snow, an old-fashioned hay ride.

★ ★ ★ ★ ★ ★

WRITE   for more information: State Board of Tourism, 865 Brook St., Rocky Hill, CT 06067.

TRY

RED FLANNEL HASH
or
CONNECTICUT BROOK TROUT
with boiled potatoes
or
SPAGHETTI WITH CLAM SAUCE, *see New Jersey*
serve with
SUCCOTASH, *see New Jersey*
BLUEBERRY PIE

Thrifty New England housewives often used up Sunday's boiled dinner on Monday with:

RED FLANNEL HASH

⅓ c minced onion	1 can (12 oz.) corned beef
¼ c butter or margarine	⅓ c milk
3 c cooked potatoes, diced	salt and pepper, to taste
1 (16 oz.) can beets, drained	1 or 2 drops hot pepper sauce

Saute onion in butter or margarine in skillet until tender. Add rest of ingredients and toss to mix well. Spread evenly in pan. Cover and cook over medium heat until brown crust forms.

Connecticut Fish Fries were such a popular event that a street in Hartford was named Fish Fry Street. A reader of Linda Giuca, food editor of the Hartford Courant — America's oldest continuously published newspaper (since 1764) — shares this recipe.

CONNECTICUT BROOK TROUT

4 to 6 (12-inch to 10-inch) trout, cleaned, with head and tail removed

1 c flour	1 T paprika
1½ t salt	1 (12 oz.) can beer
¼ t pepper	oil for frying

Cut trout into 3 or 4 pieces, crosswise. Mix together rest of ingredients except oil and blend well. Put about ½ cup of flour in a shallow bowl and roll trout pieces in it, then dip into batter. Heat cooking oil, one inch deep, in a heavy frying pan to a very hot temperature. Fry batter-dipped fish until golden brown.

★ Rita Conlin, Hartford, CT

Blueberries are ripe in Connecticut from July until late August. Another reader of the Hartford Courant sends this recipe for:

DOWN EAST BLUEBERRY PIE

½ to 1 c sugar depending on sweetness desired

¾ c water	¼ t salt
3 T flour	1 qt. blueberries, fresh or frozen
1 9-inch pie shell, baked	

Combine sugar and water in a medium saucepan. Boil for 5 minutes. Mix flour and salt with ¼ cup cold water to make a paste. Stir into sugar solution. Add half the berries. Cook slowly, stirring often, until thickened. Stir in remaining berries and pour into pie shell. Chill at least three hours. Top with whipped cream or ice cream, if desired. 6 servings.

★ Mary Lou Pierro, Manchester, CT

DELAWARE — THE FIRST STATE

Capital	Dover
Elevation	sea level to 442 ft.
Population (1980)	602,000
(1990)	633,000
1st State	admitted Dec. 7, 1787
Tree	American Holly
Flower	Peach Blossom
Bird	Blue Hen Chicken

WHILE IN DELAWARE...

CAMP   in one of 11 State Parks, including Bellevue -- beautifully wooded and landscaped former estate of the William du Ponts.

PICNIC   in the other six Parks, including Bellevue — beautifully wooded and landscaped former estate of the William du Ponts.

FISH   in Delaware Bay, or try your luck in over 30 state-owned millponds teeming with panfish, pickerel and bass.

WANDER   through many House and Garden Museums. Winterthur has over 200 furnished rooms, and 50,000 American decorative art objects from 1640 to 1840.

FOLLOW   the Heritage Trail in New Castle, with its cobblestone streets and gracious historic buildings.

WALK   across a glass floor at the Museum of Natural History to see a section of Australia's Great Barrier Reef.

VISIT   the unique Agricultural Museum, preserving Delaware's farming heritage with exhibit areas and historic structures.

★ ★ ★ ★ ★ ★

WRITE   for more information: Delaware Tourism Office, P.O. Box 1401, Dover, DE 19901. Or call 1-800-441-8846 (out of state), 1-800-282-8667 (in Delaware).

TRY

STEAMED CLAMS
or
DELAWARE CRAB CAKES
or
CHICKEN GABRIELLA, see *Washington*
serve with:
MASHED POTATOES
GREEN BEAN AND ONION SALAD
WATERMELON (if in season)
APPLESAUCE & COOKIES (if not)

While Delaware's cuisine is a blend of both southern and northern cooking, favorites are seafood, and a typical Delaware touch is the liberal amount of pepper in:

DELAWARE CRAB CAKES

1 egg	1 (7½ oz.) can crab meat,
½ c soda crackers	drained, flaked and
⅓ c milk	cartilege removed
½ t dry mustard	1 T parsley (or 1 t dry)
¼ t pepper	3 T shortening
1/8 t cayenne	Lemon wedges

Beat egg in a medium bowl; stir in crackers, milk and seasonings. Add crab meat and parsley, mixing well. Shape into patties, cover and chill for 30 minutes or more. (The patties keep their shape better when chilled.) Heat shortening in large skillet, then cook patties over medium heat until golden brown on both sides, about 3 to 4 minutes per side. Best served immediately, with lemon wedges. 5 patties.

Hard clams, one of the preferred shellfish in Delaware, are found abundantly in sections of Indian River, Rehoboth and Little Assawoman Bays. No license is required although laws govern the size and numbers of shellfish taken. If you're lucky enough to find some, try:

STEAMED CLAMS

Thoroughly wash 2 dozen clams in the shell. Let stand 15 minutes in ocean water, or brine made with ⅓ cup salt to 1 gallon cold water. Rinse. Soak again two more times.

Pour 1 cup hot water in a large kettle with a rack. (No rack? Punch holes in an aluminum pie pan — the kind frozen pies come in.) Pile the clams on the rack, cover kettle tightly and steam just until shells open. This takes about 5 to 10 minutes. Serve in shell with melted butter. 4 to 6 servings.

GREEN BEAN AND ONION SALAD

Drain one (16 oz.) can cut green beans; add one small onion, chopped. Toss with your favorite dressing.

DISTRICT OF COLUMBIA — U.S. CAPITAL
(coextensive with the City of Washington)

Population (1980) 631,000
(1990) 626,000
Tree Scarlet Oak
Flower American Beauty Rose
Bird Wood Thrush
National Bird Bald Eagle

WHILE IN WASHINGTON, D.C....

CAMP   in a neighboring state, since facilities for this activity of land travelers are non-existent in our seat of government.

TOUR   famous historical sites: Lincoln and Jefferson Memorials, Washington Monument, Ford's Theater, Lincoln Museum, Frederick Douglass' Home.

TAKE   the kids to the National Zoological Park featuring Giant Pandas Ling Ling and Hsing Hsing, gifts of the Chinese government.

SPEND   days in the Capital's Museums: National Gallery of Art, Walter Reed Medical, Capitol Children's, Dolls' House and Toy, Smithsonian (several).

SIGN   up for guided tours of the U.S. Capitol, home of Congress; the White House, home of every president since 1800.

VISIT   the Tidal Basin and the National Mall for concerts and festivals: Military Bands, Cherry Blossom, Pageant of Peace, Fourth of July.

ENJOY   a tour of John F. Kennedy Center for the Performing Arts where five theaters present superior theater, dance, film and music.

★ ★ ★ ★ ★ ★

WRITE   for more information: District of Columbia Chamber of Commerce, Suite 603, 1411 K Street, N.W., Washington, D.C. 20005. You will need to send a self-addressed stamped envelope (11 x 14 @ $2.90) for the beautifully illustrated 4-color Washington, D.C. Visitor's Guide which contains information on restaurants, hotels, calendar of events, attractions, special children's activities, maps of neighborhoods and the metropolitan area transit authority and much more.

TRY

SENATE BEAN SOUP
or
HOT DOGS IN A CORN BLANKET
with CARROT AND RAISIN SALAD, see Utah
or
YOUR CHOICE, see any state
serve with
YOUR CHOICE SALADS, VEGETABLES, ETC. see any state
PATRIOTIC PUDDING

With Congressmen from every state in the Union and Ambassadors representing their countries in this city, Washington cookery is more universal than regional. However, one continuing tradition is the bean soup, served daily in the Senate Dining Room. An easy campers' version with a similar flavor is:

SENATE BEAN SOUP

2 celery stalks, chopped	1 (16 oz.) can navy beans
½ med. onion, chopped	(may use pinto beans)
1 clove garlic, minced	1 lb. ham, cubed
1 T dried parsley flakes	salt and pepper
2½ c water	¾ c potato flakes

In a large saucepan simmer all ingredients except potato flakes for 30 minutes. Add potato flakes gradually, stirring constantly, and simmer for a few minutes. Add more water for a thinner soup, if desired. 4 servings.

If there is one food that is the symbol of America, it is the hot dog. This was emphasized when Eleanor Roosevelt served the humble sausage in a bun to the Queen and King of England. A variation is:

HOT DOGS IN A CORN BLANKET

10 hot dogs   1 pkg. cornmeal muffin mix

Line up the hot dogs in a lightly buttered 8x12 inch pan. Heat in a 400° oven while you prepare the muffin batter according to package directions. Pour the batter over the heated wieners. (The batter will not fill the pan, just be sure the wieners are covered.) Bake for 15 to 20 minutes until top is well browned.

PATRIOTIC PUDDING

Instant vanilla pudding   Blueberries
Strawberries   Whipping cream

Make pudding according to package directions. Spoon into individual bowls. When pudding is set, cover with a layer of whipped cream (or topping); place a whole strawberry in the middle and arrange blueberries in a ring around the outside.

FLORIDA — THE SUNSHINE STATE

Capital	Tallahassee
Altitude	sea level to 345 ft.
Population (1980)	9,746,000
(1990)	11,675,000
27th State	admitted March 3, 1845
Tree	Sabal Palm
Flower	Orange Blossom
Bird	Mockingbird

WHILE IN FLORIDA...

CAMP   in any of 78 State Parks, near rolling hills of citrus groves, along the calm Gulf waters, or on Atlantic beaches.

DIVE   into John Pennekamp State Park (73,130 acres all underwater) to admire a living coral reef, and swarms of brightly colored tropical fish.

EXPLORE   the mysterious Everglades where snoozing alligators, water birds and wild deer are part of nature's show in this subtropical wilderness.

VISIT   this state's largest city, Jacksonville, with magnolia-lined streets; St. Augustine, oldest city in the U.S., Kennedy Space Center and the nearby U.S. Astronaut Hall of Fame.

THRILL   to Disney World and EPCOT attractions. Take in the Ringling Museum of Art, Universal Studios, Busch Gardens theme park or admire water skiers and exotic plants in Cypress Gardens.

DRIVE   along the world's longest ocean-going road (100 miles) through the Florida Keys where lobsters may be caught — by hand, slat trap or net.

FISH   in lakes and rivers for bass, pickerel, swordfish; or tangle with a sailfish or marlin in the Atlantic; or try for red drum, tarpon and snapper in the Gulf.

★ ★ ★ ★ ★ ★

WRITE   for more information: Florida Attractions Association, P.O. Box 10295, Tallahassee, FL 32302.

TRY

ORANGE SAUCED HAM STEAKS
with yams
or
POTATO-SHRIMP SALAD
or
SAUTEED POMPANO, see *Texas*
serve with
HOT BUTTERED GREEN BEANS
KEY LIME PIE

Since Florida is noted for its oranges, we HAVE to start with a recipe using that delicious fruit.

ORANGE SAUCED HAM STEAK

4 to 6 slices ham (one serving each)
Fresh oranges   Whole cloves

Put ham in cold skillet. Slice oranges about ¼ inch thick, place one or two on each ham slice and anchor with whole cloves. Squeeze the juice from one large orange over ham (to cover bottom of pan). Arrange yam slices around and over ham. Cook slowly over low heat until all is heated through (about 10-15 minutes). 4 to 6 servings.

Nearly half the nation's shrimp supply is shipped from Florida.

POTATO-SHRIMP SALAD

¾ c mayonnaise
1 to 1½ T lemon juice
1 T prepared mustard
Salt and pepper

2 to 2½ c boiled potatoes
2 to 2½ c cooked shrimp
½ c celery, finely chopped

Combine first three ingredients in serving bowl. Add salt and pepper to your taste. Add rest of ingredients and toss. Serve on shredded lettuce and garnish with hard-cooked eggs, if desired. 4 to 6 servings.

The most flavorful of limes grow on the Florida keys, from Miami to Fort Meyers, and do not do well in other citrus regions. A true KEY Lime Pie is not named for the area, but is one made from these special Key limes.

KEY LIME PIE

3 egg yolks
1 can (14 oz.) sweetened condensed milk
⅔ c lime juice

½ t grated lime rind
Few drops green food coloring (optional)
1 baked 9-inch pie shell*

Beat egg yolks lightly and combine with condensed milk just until mixed. Add lime juice and rind and blend well. Add food coloring. Pour into baked pie shell. Filling is soft and needs to be chilled 4 hours or overnight.

Top with whipped cream, or a meringue made from the leftover whites, beaten with 4 tablespoons sugar. Spread the meringue completely over the pie, and bake at 350° for 10 minutes.

*You can make a pastry or graham cracker crust (or buy one ready-baked from the freezer section of a super market).

GEORGIA — THE PEACH STATE

Capital	Atlanta
Altitude	sea level to 4784 ft.
Population (1980)	5,463,000
(1990)	6,104,000
4th State	admitted Jan. 2, 1788
Tree	Live Oak
Flower	Cherokee Rose
Bird	Thrasher

WHILE IN GEORGIA ...

CAMP   in 44 State Parks, including Franklin D. Roosevelt State Park at Warm Springs with a Museum and his "Little White House".

MARVEL   at acres of ancient Indian Petroglyphs, restored plantations, camellia and azalea gardens, or the oldest gorge in North America.

EXPLORE   the trembling islands of tangled weeds in eerie Okefenokee Swamp, or Chattahoochee National Forest where the Appalachian trail begins.

WANDER   through Savannah's 2½ square miles of 1100 restored buildings, including the birthplace of Juliette Gordon Low, Girl Scout founder.

ATTEND   a Craft Fair, tour one of 200 carpet mills, or see the world's largest peanut-shelling plant.

SQUINT   at the capitol dome in Atlanta, sheeted with Georgia gold, then shop and stroll at Underground Atlanta.

FISH   in reservoirs, streams and lakes for trout, bream, bass and more. Saltwater fish include flounder, spotted sea trout, tarpon, Spanish mackerel.

★ ★ ★ ★ ★ ★

WRITE   for more information: Division of Tourism, 285 Peachtree Center Avenue, Atlanta, GA 30303.

TRY

COUNTRY CAPTAIN CHICKEN
or
CRAB PATTIES
or
TROUT, EISENHOWER STYLE, see *Colorado*
serve with:
BOILED RICE
CARROT STICKS
FRESH PEACHES

This popular regional dish is believed to have been brought to Georgia in colonial days by the captain of a spice-cargo ship — hence the name.

COUNTRY CAPTAIN CHICKEN

1 fryer, cut up	1 t ginger
6 T flour	2 T oil
1 t salt	

Put flour and seasonings in a bag. Shake fryer pieces to coat. Brown chicken on all sides in oil, while you make the sauce.

CURRY SAUCE

¼ c chopped onion	2 T catsup
1 T oil	1 T lemon juice
1½ t curry powder	1 T flour
1 t sugar	¼ c almonds, optional
¾ c hot water	¼ c currants, optional
1 chicken bouillon cube	2 T coconut, optional

Cook onion in oil in a heavy saucepan until limp. Add curry powder, sugar, hot water and bouillon cube. Bring to a boil, then simmer while you mix catsup, lemon juice and flour together into a smooth paste. Add flour mixture slowly to the sauce and simmer until thickened. Add any or all of optional garnishes.

Spread half of sauce over browned chicken, cover and cook for about 20 minutes. Turn chicken pieces over, pour on rest of sauce and continue cooking (covered) over low heat for 20 minutes or until chicken is done. Check occasionally — may need to add water.

Georgia ships quantities of shrimp and crab from its Atlantic coastline. Of course, some of them stay in the local market, so pick up a crab and try this typical dish.

CRAB PATTIES

1 lb. crabmeat	½ t marjoram, optional
1½ c soft breadcrumbs	¼ c mayonnaise
1 egg, slightly beaten	¼ t Worcestershire sauce
3 green onions, chopped	½ c oil

Combine all ingredients. Mix well, then knead and shape into 2-inch balls. Flatten into patties. Heat oil in a large frying pan and brown patties about 3 to 5 minutes for each side. Drain on paper towels. Serves 4 to 6.

FRESH PEACHES

Georgia is famous for its peaches. Enjoy them sliced, topped with cream, half and half, whipped cream, or ice cream.

HAWAII — THE ALOHA STATE

Capital	Honolulu
Elevation	sea level to 13,796 ft.
Population (1980)	965,000
(1990)	1,062,000
50th State	admitted Aug. 21, 1959
Tree	Candlenut
Flower	Hibiscus
Bird	Nene (Hawaiian goose)

WHILE IN HAWAII ...

CAMP in any of Six Islands' designated State Parks, or Beach Parks in the County Park System. (RV's may be rented.)

DRIVE from Waikiki Beach past Diamond Head to the Polynesian Cultural Center, made up of native South Pacific villages.

VISIT Pearl Harbor and the U.S.S. Arizona Memorial; worship in your own way at Punchbowl (Puowaina) National Memorial of the Pacific.

ENJOY all the Islands, "hopping" by scheduled Inter-Island or Air-Taxi flights from Honolulu International Airport, "Hub of the Pacific".

TOUR the East-West Center, well known for its cultural and academic interchange among peoples of the United States, Pacific and Asia.

FISH the Kona Coast for "Big Ones" on the Big Island; also view the only American soil where coffee (Kona) is raised.

CALL Aloha when you leave, remembering how you danced the Hawaiian Hula, Japanese Bon, Filipino Stick, but merely watched the Wild Tahitians.

★ ★ ★ ★ ★ ★ ★

WRITE for more information: Hawaii Visitors Bureau, Suite 801, Waikiki Business Plaza, 2270 Kalakaua Ave., Honolulu, HI 96815.

For camping information, write to Muriel A. Anderson, Office of Tourism, P.O. Box 2359, Honolulu, HI 96804.

TRY

HONOLULU PORK AND PINEAPPLE
or
CHICKEN TERIYAKI
or
SHRIMP EGG FOO YUNG with QUICK CHINESE SAUCE
serve with
HOT RICE
GREEN AND GOLD SALAD, *see California*
SLICED FRESH PINEAPPLE

Think Hawaii and envision a luau — the complicated roasting of a whole pig in a pit lined with Ti leaves, accompanied with vegetables. You can achieve a similar taste with:

HONOLULU PORK AND PINEAPPLE

6 pork chops	½ green pepper, thinly sliced
salt and pepper	
1 (20 oz.) can pineapple chunks, undrained	1 clove garlic, minced
	1 c celery, diagonally sliced
½ c onion, chopped	

Trim fat from chops. Use a piece of fat to grease the bottom of a heavy frying pan. Brown chops on both sides, drain off fat. Lightly season chops with salt and pepper. Add remaining ingredients except celery; cover and cook 2 or 3 minutes. Add celery and simmer for 15-20 minutes until chops are done. If mixture seems dry at any time, add a small amount of water.

The Japanese brought teriyaki sauce to the Islands.

CHICKEN TERIYAKI

½ c soy sauce	1 t ginger
½ c water	½ t garlic powder
¼ c dry sherry	2 t vinegar
¼ c brown sugar	2½-3 lb. fryer pieces

Pour soy sauce, water and sherry into a large skillet. Add rest of ingredients and stir to blend. Place chicken pieces in pan, cover and simmer for 30 minutes. Turn chicken pieces, and continue simmering for another 30 minutes. 4-6 servings

Among many other tasty vegetables, the Chinese introduced bean sprouts to Hawaii.

SHRIMP EGG FOO YUNG

1 lb. fresh bean sprouts, chopped to reduce length	2 (4½ oz.) can shrimps
	¾ t salt
3 or 4 green onions, including tops, chopped	6 eggs

In a large bowl, combine all ingredients except eggs. Add eggs and stir only until well mixed. Do NOT beat. Pour egg mixture (about ¼ c at a time) into well-oiled skillet, spreading into 4-inch cakes. Cook over moderate heat until cakes are lightly browned. Serve with QUICK CHINESE SAUCE: In a small saucepan, heat ½ teaspoon chicken bouillon granules in ½ cup water; add 1 teaspoon sugar and 1 teaspoon vinegar. Stir 1½ tablespoon cornstarch into 1 tablespoon soy sauce; add to bouillon mixture, cooking and stirring until smooth and thickened. 4 servings, 3 cakes per person.

IDAHO — THE GEM STATE

Capital	Boise
Elevation	710 ft. to 12,662 ft.
Population (1980)	944,000
(1990)	1,062,000
43rd State	admitted July 3, 1890
Flower	Syringa
Bird	Mountain Bluebird

WHILE IN IDAHO...

CAMP   in the natural beauty first seen by Lewis and Clark over a century ago. Choose from 22 State Parks of all descriptions.

VIEW   North America's deepest gorge, Hell's Canyon, accessible by float boat, or let your eyes climb the Sawtooth or Tetons of America's Alps.

CHOOSE   among many Powwows, Festivals and Rodeos put on by the Shoshone, Blackfoot, Owyhee and Nez Perce Tribes.

SKI   most anywhere but notably world-famous Sun Valley; then see Mammoth Ice Caves and Shoshone Falls, "Niagara of the West."

TAKE   an excursion boat ride on beautiful Lake Coeur d'Alene; motor to an awe-inspiring scenic experience at Lake Pend Oreille.

BROWSE   in any of three dozen museums to find some of the 80 varieties of gemstones found within the "Gem State".

EXPLORE   scenic Island Park on your way to easily accessible Yellowstone and Grand Teton National Parks and the famous Jackson Hole country.

★ ★ ★ ★ ★ ★

WRITE   for more information: Idaho Travel Council, 700 W. State Street, Boise, ID 83720 or call 1-800-635-7820.

TRY

BRAISED VENISON LOIN CHOPS
or
PORK CHOPS WITH STUFFING
or
MORMON SPLIT PEA SOUP, see Utah
serve with
SUNSHINE SALAD, see Montana
BAKED IDAHO POTATOES
FRESH BING CHERRIES

Deer are plentiful in Idaho, but if you're not a hunter, or don't have a friend who is, you can substitute beef.

BRAISED VENISON LOIN CHOPS

4 medium loin chops	1 med. onion, chopped
¼ t garlic **powder**	½ c red wine
salt and pepper	2 T flour
½ lb. sliced mushrooms	½ c milk
or 1 (8 oz.) can	½ c sour cream

Heat oil in a Dutch Oven, or electric skillet. Season chops with garlic powder, dust with flour and brown in hot oil. Remove chops and set aside. Saute mushrooms and onions in same pan for one or two minutes, until barely tender. Return chops, pour wine over. Simmer, covered, 5 to 10 minutes.

Mix 2 tablespoons flour with a little of the milk; add rest of milk and sour cream. Push chops to one side and stir flour mixture into pan gravy. Cook and stir until thickened, rearrange chops, cover and simmer (do **not** boil) 15 to 20 minutes. 2-4 servings.

★ Pat and Larry Boal, Pine Grove, CA

Lumberjacks in Idaho might have enjoyed a hearty meal such as:

PORK CHOPS WITH STUFFING

6 lean pork chops	1 apple, peeled & chopped
1 (6 oz.) pkg. top of stove poultry dressing	2 T onion, minced
	½ t sage

In a 10-inch round frypan, brown 3 pork chops on one side only. Remove, and brown the other three chops on both sides, while you prepare stuffing according to package directions. Return the first three pork chops to frying pan, placing browned side up. Stir apple, onion and sage into stuffing; spread over chops in pan. Top with remaining chops. Cover and cook over low heat about 15 minutes. 6 servings.

No Idaho meal would be complete without an Idaho potato. These famous russets were developed by the plant wizard, Luther Burbank, and are best baked, served with butter and a dash of sweet cream.

ILLINOIS — THE PRAIRIE STATE

Capital	Springfield
Elevation	279 ft. to 1235 ft.
Population (1980)	11,448,000
(1990)	11,552,000
21st state	admitted Dec. 3, 1818
Tree	Oak
Flower	Violet
Bird	Cardinal

WHILE IN ILLINOIS...

CAMP in State Parks — Starved Rock with its geologic wonders and French and Indian history, Chain of Lakes, Illinois Beach, or Pere Marquette.

FLOAT down the mighty Mississippi, canoe a smaller river, explore the Shawnee National Forest, or Wildlife Prairie Park.

FISH for over 190 native species in thousands of streams, rivers, lakes. Salmon, introduced for ecological reasons, are thriving in Lake Michigan.

FOLLOW Abraham Lincoln lore from the village in New Salem to Springfield where his presence pervades the many sites and exhibits in his memory.

VISIT pre-historic Indian mounds, Amish colonies, restored pioneer villages, towns filled with grand homes of the Victorian period.

MARVEL at Chicago's attractions: park-lined lakefront, innovative architecture, Sears Tower — the world's tallest building, zoos, museums, The Loop, The Magnificent Mile.

TOUR industries from potteries to a four-story freezer containing 8 million cakes, from farm implements to catalogue craft items.

★ ★ ★ ★ ★ ★

WRITE for more information: Illinois Office of Tourism, Dept. of Commerce & Community Affairs, 620 E. Adams St., Springfield, IL 62701.

TRY

HORSERADISH STEAK
or
SWISS HERO SANDWICH
or
SWEDISH MEATBALLS, see *Minnesota*
serve with
ALL AMERICAN POTATO SALAD
Carrots and Peas
BROWN BEARS IN THE APPLE ORCHARD, see *Indiana*

Our correspondent says that Illinois is the horseradish capital of the world!

HORSERADISH STEAK

1 sirloin steak (3 lb., 2-inch thick)
1½ T lemon juice
1 - 3 T grated fresh horseradish (to taste)
1½ T Worcestershire sauce
¾ c chili sauce

Slash edges of steak. Pierce holes in steak with fork. Combine marinade ingredients in plastic bag and let steak marinate in it for at least one hour. When ready to cook, pour marinade into a cup. Place steak on hot grill brushed with oil to prevent sticking, about 6 inches from hot coals. Brush with marinade. Cook until browned on bottom, then turn, brush with marinade and grill until done to your taste. Serves 4 to 6.

★ Shirley Russell, Chicago, IL

Illinois leads the nation in the production of Swiss cheese. This sandwich combines the German and Swiss heritage of the state.

SWISS HERO SANDWICH

Any variety of German sausage, thinly sliced

Slices of Swiss cheese French rolls
Shredded lettuce   Pickles   Mayonnaise and mustard

Split rolls, put mayonnaise on one side, and mustard on the other (to suit your taste). Alternate layers of sausage and cheese slices on bottom of roll, until as plump as desired. Add pickles and lettuce; cover with top of roll; press together lightly.

ALL-AMERICAN POTATO SALAD

¼ c mayonnaise
1 t salt
1 t prepared mustard
1 T vinegar
3 T pickle relish (optional)
4 medium cooked potatoes, diced
4 hard-cooked eggs, chopped
1 c celery, chopped
1 onion, finely chopped

In a large bowl mix together the first five ingredients. Stir in the potatoes, and let marinate while you prepare the rest of the ingredients. Now stir all together gently and serve cool, but not chilled.

NOTE: if cucumbers are available, add one cubed for extra crunch.

INDIANA — THE HOOSIER STATE

Capital	Indianapolis
Elevation	320 ft. to 1257 ft.
Population (1980)	5,471,000
(1990)	5,504,000
19th state	admitted Dec. 11, 1816
Tree	Tulip
Flower	Peony
Bird	Cardinal

WHILE IN INDIANA...

CAMP in Indiana's numerous State parks and forests, including Indiana Dunes on Lake Michigan and Clifty Falls with a 400 foot bluff.

VISIT Lincoln Boyhood National Monument, which preserves Abraham Lincoln's childhood home, now a living farm with costumed guides.

FISH in rivers, lakes and reservoirs. In the winter ice-skate, sled or ski in many of the same regions.

EXPLORE caves and caverns, including Bluespring Caverns containing America's longest navigable underground river.

TOUR museums, featuring railroad depots to pioneer cabins, antique phonographs to vintage cars, "Circus City" to glass blowing.

ROAR with the crowd at the racing event of the year — the famous Indianapolis "500" mile race.

JOIN in a festival — dozens each month — from New Year's Open House at President Harrison's home to the living Christmas Pageant.

★ ★ ★ ★ ★ ★

WRITE for more information: State Board of Tourism, One N. Capitol #700, Indianapolis, IN 46204.

TRY

SAUSAGE WITH HOMINY
or
MAPLE SPARERIBS
with baked potatoes
or
SUE'S CHICKEN POT PIE, see *South Dakota*
serve with:
GREEN SALAD
BROWN BEARS IN THE APPLE ORCHARD

34

Corn was always the first crop planted by the pioneers from the eastern seaboard who settled the Old Northwest Territory. Pigs were brought in early and adapted themselves well to the wild surroundings, even killing and eating rattlesnakes with no ill effects to themselves, or the settlers who ate them.

SAUSAGE WITH HOMINY

1 lb. pork sausage links   1 (12 oz.) can tomatoes
1 (12 oz.) can hominy   Salt and pepper, to taste

Brown sausage, pour off excess fat. Drain hominy and add to sausage. Stir in tomatoes. Simmer gently until most liquid is gone. Add salt and pepper.

In early March, Indiana invites visitors to watch the harvesting of maple syrup in three towns. Even if you can't watch the process, you can enjoy the maple flavor in these grilled or baked ribs.

MAPLE SPARERIBS

3 to 4 lb. of pork spareribs

Sauce

¾ c maple syrup   1 T prepared mustard
4 T catsup   1 t garlic salt

Mix sauce ingredients and blend well.

To grill: Place ribs over hot coals and grill about 30 minutes, turning once or twice. Spread out the coals, or raise the grill, for slower cooking. Baste with sauce, then cook for another 30 to 45 minutes, turning and basting several times until ribs are glazed.

To bake: Roast in a large, shallow pan in 400° oven for 30 minutes. Pour off fat. Reduce oven temperature to 350°; pour sauce over ribs and continue to roast, basting frequently, for about 45 minutes.

This favorite dessert of Girl Scout outings is in memory of a famous American, Johnny Appleseed, who is buried at Fort Wayne, Indiana, in a park bearing his name.

BROWN BEARS IN THE APPLE ORCHARD

1 (16 oz.) can applesauce   ½ pkg. Gingerbread Mix
    ½ c water

Spread applesauce over the bottom of a frying pan. Stir together gingerbread mix and water (½ package is a scant one cup). Drop batter into applesauce and cook over low heat until top looks dry. Serve fruit side up, hot or cold.

IOWA — THE HAWKEYE STATE

Capital	Des Moines
Elevation	480 ft. to 2,852 ft.
Population (1980)	2,914,000
(1990)	2,851,000
29th State	admitted Dec. 28, 1846
Tree	Oak
Flower	Wild Rose
Bird	Eastern Goldfinch

WHILE IN IOWA ...

CAMP and be assured of something for everyone in a choice of 111 State Parks, Forests and Recreation Areas.

TRAVEL through tall corn fields, whose annual bushel basket yield, put side-by-side would stretch 12½ times around the world.

VISIT Pella for Old World Dutch charm and seven Amana Colonies for examples of Swiss and German thrift and hard work.

JOIN in plowing with oxen and the activities of traditional craftsmen from early times to the present at Living History Farms.

FIND the Effigy Mounds in shapes of birds and animals. Discover a nesting place of the American Bald Eagle along the Mississippi.

THRILL to pari-mutuel greyhound and horse racing, and riverboat casinos.

FISH well-stocked trout creeks, the interior streams; or the boundary rivers, Missouri and Mississippi, for walleye, crappie, bass and catfish.

★ ★ ★ ★ ★ ★

WRITE for more information: Iowa Department of Economic Development, Division of Tourism, 200 East Grand, Des Moines, IA 50309.

TRY
WIENER SCHNITZEL
or
LUNCHEON MEAT BARBECUE
or
CRISPY FRIED FISH, *see Alabama*
serve with
BUTTERED NOODLES
HOT CABBAGE SLAW, *see Kansas*
SLICED TOMATOES, ONIONS AND CUCUMBERS
HONEY POPCORN SQUARES

Settling along Iowa river towns in the early 1800's, German-Austrian immigrants' fondness for veal added Breaded Veal Cutlets to the American cuisine, called originally:

WIENER SCHNITZEL

2 lbs. veal steak, chops, or cutlets*
flour　　　　　　　　　　1 c dry breadcrumbs
1 egg　　　　　　　　　　salt and pepper
¼ c water　　　　　　　　oil for frying
　　　　　　　　　　　　lemon juice

　　Cut veal into serving pieces. Dust with flour, then dip in fork-whipped egg mixed with water. Coat with breadcrumbs and brown in hot oil on both sides. Cover and cook slowly for 20 minutes then remove cover and allow to crisp, turning once, for about 10 minutes. Sprinkle lightly with lemon juice when serving. 6 servings.
　　*If veal is unavailable, try ground turkey meat. Shape into ¼-inch patties and proceed as above.

Iowa is first in the number of hogs raised and processed (24% of the U.S. supply), and meat processing and distribution is a major industry. Try a canned meat in:

LUNCHEON MEAT BARBECUE

½ c chopped onion　　　　2 T brown sugar
2 T oil　　　　　　　　　½ c water
1 can luncheon meat　　　　3 T vinegar
1 c catsup　　　　　　　　1 T prepared mustard

　　Cook onion in oil until golden. Cut luncheon meat into thick slices. Add to onion with rest of ingredients. Simmer 15 minutes, to blend flavors. 4-6 servings (depends on how thick you slice the meat).

Iowa is a top popcorn producer, with the world's largest corn cribs, holding 4,000,000 tons of popcorn, in Sioux City.

HONEY POPCORN SQUARES

8 c popped corn　　　　　　1 c honey

　　In a small, heavy saucepan, heat honey to hard ball stage. Pour over popcorn, mixing well. (Be sure to scrape the bottom — the honey tends to slip through). With buttered hands, press into a 9x13 buttered baking dish. Cut into squares when cool. Keep airtight to retain crispness.

KANSAS — THE SUNFLOWER STATE

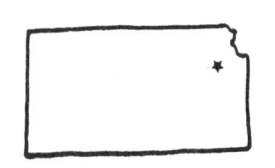

Capital	Topeka
Elevation	680 ft. to 4039 ft.
Population (1980)	2,364,000
(1990)	2,460,000
34th State	admitted Jan. 29, 1861
Tree	Cottonwood
Flower	Sunflower
Bird	Meadowlark
Insect	Honeybee

WHILE IN KANSAS ...

CAMP at any of 24 State Parks where you can enjoy full hook-ups or a more primitive site for just roughing it.

TRAVEL the Santa Fe Trail and visit some of the Forts along the way, well-known to Indian tribes and wagon train pioneers.

STOP in Dodge City, known as "The Cowboy Capital of the World", and discover at Boot Hill Museum why it claims that fame.

VISIT the Kansas Cosmosphere, "Little Sweden U.S.A.", Johnson Safari Museum, Eisenhower Center, and the "Waldorf of the Prairies".

TAKE your pick of monthly Festivals: numerous ethnic, music — from Bluegrass to Classical, Pancake Races, Threshing Bees, Indian Peace Treaty.

SEE the Agricultural Hall of Fame, honoring people and events which made Kansas known as the "Bread Basket of the World".

FISH for walleye, catfish, striped bass in well-stocked city, county, and state lakes; and in 20 big federal reservoirs.

★ ★ ★ ★ ★ ★ ★

WRITE for more information: Kansas Dept. of Commerce, Travel and Tourism Division, 400 SW 8th, Suite 500, Topeka, KS 66603. Or call: 1-800-2 KANSAS.

TRY

CHUCKWAGON SKILLET
or
CHICKEN 'N NOODLES
or
PAN BARBECUED SPARERIBS, see Arizona
serve with
KANSAS CORN ON THE COB
HOT CABBAGE SLAW
COVERED WAGON CANDY, see Utah

Although the great era of cattle drives across the dusty Midwest plains from Texas to Kansas spanned only about two decades, the appeal of Chuckwagon Chow has lingered on:

CHUCKWAGON SKILLET

4 slices bacon	¼ t marjoram leaves, salt and pepper
½ c chopped green pepper	2 (19 oz.) cans Chunky Beef Soup
½ c chopped onion	

Cook bacon in skillet until crisp; drain bacon on paper towels, and pour off all but 1 tablespoon drippings. (Save 3 tablespoons for Hot Cabbage Slaw). Stir onions, green pepper and seasonings in remaining fat in skillet, and cook slowly until lightly browned. Add undiluted soup, stirring over low heat until hot and thickened. Dish up on plates and sprinkle wih crumbled bacon. 4 servings.

When early-day Kansans gathered for Threshing Bees, as many as 50 people had to be fed three meals a day. Homemade noodles and chickens that were caught, cleaned and stewed were combined into this dish, made easy for you with prepared foods.

CHICKEN 'N NOODLES

1 small onion, chopped	salt and pepper
2 T oil	2 T flour
6 c chicken broth	¼ c cold water
3 med. carrots, thinly sliced	1 can chunked chicken
	2 c uncooked noodles

In a large kettle, saute the onion in the oil; add chicken broth and bring to boiling. Add carrots and noodles, season; cover and simmer for 10 minutes. Combine flour with cold water into a thin paste; add to the vegetable-noodle mixture, stirring and cooking until slightly thickened. Mix in the chicken and heat through. 4 servings.

HOT CABBAGE SLAW

1 small head cabbage	1 egg
salt and pepper	¼ c vinegar, diluted with ¼ c water
1 t sugar	
3 T bacon grease	

Shred, or finely chop cabbage. Stir into bacon grease, melted in a medium saucepan. Add seasonings, cover and cook over low heat, stirring occasionally for about five minutes. Meanwhile, beat egg slightly, add diluted vinegar and stir together. Pour over cabbage; cook a minute or two longer. 4 servings.

KENTUCKY — THE BLUEGRASS STATE

Capital	Frankfort
Elevation	257 ft. to 4145 ft.
Population (1980)	3,660,777
(1990)	3,685,000
15th State	admitted June 1, 1792
Tree	Kentucky Coffee Tree
Flower	Goldenrod
Bird	Cardinal

WHILE IN KENTUCKY...

CAMP in a State Park, all with children's playgrounds. Most have pool, river or lake swimming; game courts for basketball and badminton through shuffleboard and volleyball; some with tennis courts and golf courses.

VISIT Abraham Lincoln's Birthplace Cabin; his boyhood home in Knob Creek; the actual cabin where his mother was courted by his father.

MARVEL at the world's longest cave system in Mammoth Cave National Park; or tour smaller ones, including Diamond Caverns and Mammoth Onyx Cave.

ATTEND the week-long Kentucky Derby Festival or admire the 35 breeds of horses at the Kentucky Horse Park, home of the International Museum of the Horse.

WANDER through Fort Boonesborough, settled by Daniel Boone in the 1700s; Shaker Village of Pleasant Hill; or Stephen Foster's "Old Kentucky Home."

SPEND some time on the lakes in sailboats, fishing boats, pontoons or houseboats. Or you can choose canoeing down a smooth stream or rafting on a mountain river with whitewater up to Class V.

FISH year-round in lakes or rivers for bass, catfish, muskie, trout and various other species.

★ ★ ★ ★ ★ ★

WRITE for more information: Kentucky Department of Travel, Department MR, P.O. Box 2011, Frankfort, KY 40602. 1-800-225-TRIP, Ext. 67.

TRY

BASS FILLETS
or
CAMPERS' BURGOO
or
BATTER-FRIED CHICKEN, see *West Virginia*
serve with
JOHNNYCAKE, see *Missouri*
FRESH SLICED TOMATOES
ORANGE AMBROSIA

Kentucky Bass (sometimes called spotted bass) is the official state fish. This honored species and two other varieties of bass are available year-round.

BASS FILLETS

Coat fillets with flour or cornmeal and fry in about ¼ inch of oil or shortening in a large frying pan. Cook until golden brown on each side and fish flakes easily. Season with salt and pepper.

Fillets may be broiled. Spread both sides of fish with oil or mayonnaise and place 2 or 3 inches from heat in broiler. Cook about 3 minutes on each side. Salt and pepper and serve with lemon quarters.

Want them baked? Place fish in oiled pan (turn once to oil both sides). Add salt and pepper and pour over a cup of milk. Bake 30 to 35 minutes in a 350⁰ oven.

Political rallies in the 1800's often relied on food and drink as vote-getters. Burgoo, cooked all night in huge iron pots and served in tin cups, proved so popular that the rallies were called "Burgoos".

CAMPERS' BURGOO

½ lb. ground beef
1 med. onion, chopped
2 (10 oz.) pkg. frozen mixed vegetables
2 cooked potatoes, diced
1 (16 oz.) stewed tomatoes
2 c chicken broth
Few drops hot pepper sauce, to taste
1 c cooked chicken, chunked

(Adding 1 T lemon juice, dash cinnamon, 2 T brown sugar is optional, but gives a tangy-sweet flavor.)

Brown ground beef and onions in large skillet. Add rest of ingredients, cover and simmer about 20 minutes until vegetables are done.

Note: You may use 2 (10 oz.) cans vegetable soup or 1 (16 oz.) can mixed vegetables for frozen. Add last and heat through.

ORANGE AMBROSIA

Dice two oranges and combine with miniature marshmallows (or big ones cut in quarters). Add a handful of coconut if you have it.

Bonus hint: Pour boiling water over oranges, let stand five minutes and the white will stick to the peels, not the segments.

LOUISIANA — THE PELICAN STATE

Capital	Baton Rouge
Elevation	minus 5 ft. to 535 ft.
Population (1980)	4,205,000
(1990)	4,501,000
18th State	admitted April 30, 1812
Tree	Cypress
Flower	Magnolia
Bird	Pelican

WHILE IN LOUISIANA...

CAMP   in a State Park; all located adjacent to water — lake, river or Gulf — including Audobon Memorial State Park, a wild bird sanctuary.

JOIN   the revelers in New Orleans for the Mardi Gras carnival; listen to the Jazz on Bourbon Street, and explore the French Quarter.

STEP   into a French-accented world, Acadian Village and Vermilionville -- bayou settlements that preserve Cajun music, food, handcrafts and their joy of life.

EXPLORE   the mighty Mississippi in a sternwheeler or riverboat; bayous and marshes on skiffs or swamp boats; lakes and rivers on a side-wheeler.

FOLLOW   the Creole Nature Trail, a combination of wildflowers, magnificent oaks, indigenous animals, and the largest alligator population in North America.

TOUR   rice, sugar and cotton plantation homes, fields and gardens; an antique syrup mill; a sugar cane press; and America's oldest rice mill.

FISH   for freshwater fish, including bass, white perch, catfish. You can fish from oil rigs in the Gulf for tarpon, pompano, speckled trout and more.

★ ★ ★ ★ ★ ★

WRITE   for more information: Office of Tourism, P.O. Box 94291, Baton Rouge, LA 70804-9691. Or call: 1-800-334-8626 or 1-800-33-GUMBO.

TRY

NEW ORLEANS CREOLE GUMBO
or
CAMPERS' JAMBALAYA
or
SAUTEED POMPANO, see *Texas*
FRESH SPINACH SALAD
CRUSTY FRENCH BREAD
PURCHASED PECAN PIE or PRALINES

Creole is the name given both to the people and cookery of Louisiana, particularly of New Orleans. Gumbo is another name for okra — a podlike vegetable with thickening qualities — and stews including okra are called "Gumbo".

NEW ORLEANS CREOLE GUMBO

1 med. onion, chopped
3 T oil
1 No. 2 can okra, undrained
1 No. 2 can tomatoes
2 c water
1 t salt
1 (4½ oz.) can shrimp
1 (4½ oz.) can crabmeat
Hot cooked rice

Cook onion in oil until golden. Stir in okra, tomatoes, water and salt. Simmer for 20 minutes to blend flavors and thicken stew. Add shrimp and crab; cook gently until heated through. Put servings of hot rice into soup bowls, and pour gumbo over. 4 to 6 servings.

Of French origin, this popular Creole dish has rightfully spread across the nation. Ham, chicken, shrimp, crabmeat, oysters, and sausage can be used — alone or in combination.

CAMPERS' JAMBALAYA

¼ c minced onion
¼ c minced green pepper
2 T oil
1 (14 oz.) can tomatoes
1 t salt
dash of pepper
drop or two of cayenne
1 c cooked ham, diced
1 c diced cooked chicken
2 c INSTANT rice
2 c water

Cook onions and green pepper in oil until softened. Add rest of ingredients; bring to a boil, then reduce heat and simmer for 10 minutes, uncovered, stirring occasionally.

FRESH SPINACH SALAD

½ lb. fresh spinach, tossed with:

TANGY BACON DRESSING

4 slices bacon
¼ c vinegar
1 T sugar

Fry bacon until crisp. Remove from pan, pour off all but ¼ cup fat, then, with a fork, whisk in the vinegar and sugar. Pour over prepared spinach, carefully washed and torn into large pieces. Crumble bacon and add to salad. Toss well. Finely chopped, hard-cooked eggs may be sprinkled over the top.

MAINE — THE PINE TREE STATE

Capital	Augusta
Elevation	sea level to 5,268 ft.
Population (1980)	1,133,000
(1990)	1,173,000
23rd state	admitted March 15, 1820
Tree	Pine
Flower	Pine Cone
Bird	Chicadee

WHILE IN MAINE...

CAMP — in Acadia National Park, near Bar Harbor, a popular summer resort since the middle of the 19th century.

EXPLORE — the many State Parks, located along Maine's rocky shore, on sand beaches, islands, lakes, in forests, hills, mountains.

TOUR — textile, shoe manufacturing, glass-making plants; see how canoes are made; or visit a stove foundry.

FISH — in some of Maine's 2,500 lakes and 5,000 rivers and streams, or try some deep-sea fishing in the Atlantic.

SKI — in your choice of over 25 ski resorts, including Sugar Loaf/USA with the most dependable snow conditions in the East.

VISIT — Maine's diverse Museums, which include the Maine State House, the Museum of Stone Age Antiquities, the Marine Museum, the Gallery of Modern Art, the Shaker Museum, Railway Village and the Lumberman's Museum.

★ ★ ★ ★ ★ ★ ★

WRITE — for more information: The Maine Publicity Bureau, 97 Winthrop Street, Hallowell, ME 04347.

TRY

MAINE LOBSTER STEW
or
CORN OYSTERS
with grilled or roasted chicken
or
RED FLANNEL HASH, *see Connecticut*
serve with:
HEAD LETTUCE WITH THOUSAND ISLAND DRESSING
FRESH BERRIES

A common sight along Maine's shore is the lobsterman fixing his traps — the same kind of slatted wooden "lobster pots" used by the early settlers to catch these delicious crustaceans. At first eaten at breakfast, Lobster Stew eventually became a dinner dish, served with dill pickles and oyster crackers.

MAINE LOBSTER STEW

2 - 2½ c lobster meat 4 c milk
4 T butter 1 t salt
1 slice onion, minced ¼ t pepper

Cut lobster meat into bite-sized pieces. Saute in butter with the onion. Heat milk in separate saucepan. Add hot milk to lobster and continue heating until stew steams. Add seasonings. If a thicker stew is preferred, add a few crushed soda crackers. Serves 4-6.

When neither fish nor meat were available, the ingenious New England housewife served "Corn Oysters". These corn fritters were so named because when fried they spread to an oyster shape, with curled edges. They were served as a main dish with maple syrup. Today they make a delicious side-dish with chicken.

CORN OYSTERS

1 large egg
1 can (8 oz.) whole kernel corn, drained
Dash of salt and pepper
⅓ c flour   Oil for frying

Beat eggs well. Mix in corn and seasonings; then add flour and stir thoroughly. Heat oil in large frying pan (should be about 1/8 inch deep). Drop batter by tablespoonfuls into hot fat, and fry until golden brown on each side, turning once. Drain on paper towels.

FRESH BERRIES

In the summertime there are many berries growing in the woods or along roadways. If you don't want to pick them, buy some from children who have, or from a fruit stand. Serve with cream for a "simply" delicious dessert.

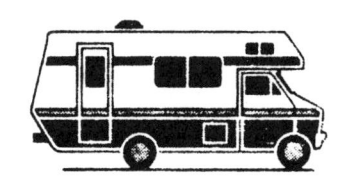

MARYLAND — THE OLD LINE STATE

Capital	Annapolis
Altitude	sea level to 3360 ft.
Population (1980)	4,216,000
(1990)	4,463,000
7th State	admitted April 28, 1788
Tree	White Oak
Flower	Black-eyed Susan
Bird	Baltimore Oriole

WHILE IN MARYLAND...

CAMP — in private campgrounds or state parks and enjoy crabbing, boating, hiking in the country, the mountains, along the seashore, or stay near a city.

RELAX — in the sun and sand of Atlantic beaches, surf-cast or deep-sea fish. Discover Assateague Island, where wild ponies run free.

HIKE — a short distance on the Appalachian Trail near Boonesboro to the first monument built to honor our nation's first president.

TOUR — the National Aquarium in Baltimore -- one of the largest and most sophisticated in the world, featuring its new Marine Mammal Pavilion.

VISIT — Fort McHenry in Baltimore where in 1812 Francis Scott Key wrote our National Anthem.

FIND — Annapolis, the U.S. Capitol of 200 years ago; walk along the seawall of the Naval Academy to admire the majesty of Chesapeake Bay.

EAT OUT — to sample the native flavor of Maryland Beaten Biscuits, Steamed Blue Crabs, Crab Cakes, and Southern Stuffed Ham.

★ ★ ★ ★ ★ ★

WRITE — for a Maryland Travel Kit: Maryland Office of Tourism Development, 217 E. Redwood St., Baltimore, MD 21202. or call: 1-800-543-1036.

TRY

BALTIMORE CRAB LOUIS
or
MARYLAND CHICKEN
or
QUICK PORCUPINE MEAT BALLS, see *Nevada*
serve with
GARLIC FRENCH BREAD
MELON FRUIT CUP

Shellfish is plentiful in all Middle Atlantic states, and is never tastier than in:

BALTIMORE CRAB LOUIS

2 (7½ oz.) cans crabmeat	½ c mayonnaise
1 med. head lettuce	½ c catsup
4 hard-cooked eggs	1 t minced onion
4 tomatoes	Olives, optional

Drain crabmeat and remove cartilege. Shred lettuce and place on four plates, top with crabmeat. Quarter eggs and tomatoes, arrange alternately around crabmeat. Mix mayonnaise, catsup and onion. Drizzle over salads. Decorate with olives. 4 servings.

Marylanders like to serve double-dipped chicken breasts with traditional garnishes — lightly fried bananas and bacon curls or fried pineapple rings and corn fritters. Not so traditional, but also good, is to place the chicken breasts on a platter of cooked noodles and pour cream gravy over all.

MARYLAND CHICKEN

4 chicken breasts	1½ c fine, dry bread or cracker crumbs
¼ c flour, seasoned with salt and pepper	3 T butter or margarine
1¼ c milk, divided	3 T oil
1 egg	1 T flour

Put ¼ cup flour in a shallow bowl, and ¼ cup milk in another. Dip chicken in milk, then in flour, shaking off any excess. Let the chicken pieces dry for 10 minutes. Fork whip an egg in the milk dish, and put breadcrumbs in the flour bowl. Dip the breasts first in the egg mixture, then in breadcrumbs — coating lightly.

Heat butter and oil in a skillet. Cook chicken breasts over low heat, turning occasionally until tender, about 20 minutes. Remove breasts to paper towels and keep warm while preparing the cream gravy.

Pour off all but 2 tablespoons pan drippings. Stir in 2 tablespoons flour, remove from heat and gradually stir in 1 cup of milk. Return to heat and cook, stirring constantly, until thick and smooth, about 2 or 3 minutes. Place chicken breasts over cooked noodles, alternating with the garnishes. 4 servings.

MELON FRUIT CUP

1 medium cantaloupe   Diced fruit

Slice cantaloupe into quarters (stem end to blossom end). Remove seeds and fill center with any diced fruit — orange, peach, pineapple, watermelon. Add a grape or two for garnish if handy.

MASSACHUSETTS — THE BAY STATE

Capital	Boston
Elevation	sea level to 3491 ft.
Population (1980)	5,737,000
(1990)	5,832,000
6th State	admitted Feb. 6, 1788
Tree	Elm
Flower	Mayflower
Bird	Chickadee

WHILE IN MASSACHUSETTS...

CAMP   in any of the 21 State Parks in this Heartland of New England and relive the history of our country's origin.

LOSE   yourself in the quiet realm of nature along the trails of the region known as the "Switzerland of America."

FEEL   the reverent thrill of Freedom from the solid decks of the USS Constitution — "Old Ironsides" and the fields of Lexington and Concord.

ENJOY   a variety of activities: Maple-sugaring, Whale Watching, Basketball Hall of Fame, Hoosac Museum, Bridge of Flowers, Pilgrim's Progress, Boston Symphony.

VIEW   the fascinating manufacture of the only paper on which U.S. currency has been printed since 1801.

FISH   fresh or salt water for a wide variety of "pole benders". Remember your visitor's permits.

AMAZE   yourselves in leisure time by compiling your own list of famous men and women whose origin was in Massachusetts.

★ ★ ★ ★ ★ ★

WRITE   for more information: Department of Tourism, 100 Cambridge St., 13th Floor, Boston, MA 02202.

TRY

CAMPERS' BAKED BEANS AND BROWN BREAD
or
CAPE COD CLAM CHOWDER
or
PAN FRIED SCROD, see *New Hampshire*
serve with:
YANKEE SLAW
SUCCOTASH, see *New Jersey*
BOSTON CREAM PIE

All through the New England states, baked beans and brown bread are a usual Saturday night supper, or a Sunday morning breakfast.

CAMPERS' BAKED BEANS AND BROWN BREAD
1 (1 lb.) can Boston Brown Bread
2 (1 lb.) cans Boston Baked Beans

Wrap the bread in foil, then heat in a 350° oven, over a charcoal fire, or in an electric skillet. (All take about 15 minutes.) Meanwhile heat the beans. Pickles are a traditional accompaniment. 4 servings.

Massachusetts cooks cut their clams in larger chunks, and prefer a thicker chowder than most other New Englanders, but no Down Easter cook will tolerate a smidgeon of tomato.

CAPE COD CLAM CHOWDER

½ c salt pork, diced*	1 c boiling water
1 small onion, chopped	2 c milk
3 c diced raw potatoes	salt and pepper
1 (7 oz.) can clams	soda crackers

Brown salt pork and onions. Add potatoes, water and seasonings. Cook until potatoes are tender, about 20 minutes. Add undrained clams and milk; heat until almost boiling. Thicken with crushed crackers. 4 servings.

*4 slices bacon, cut fine, may be substituted, but won't give quite the traditional flavor.

Coleslaw is often served with baked beans in the Bay State, and this tangy-sweet dressing makes it a typical:

YANKEE SLAW

1 c milk, divided	¼ c vinegar
1½ T flour	1 egg
½ t salt	2 T sugar
1 T prepared mustard	1 T butter or margarine

1 medium head cabbage, shredded

Scald ¾ c milk. Make a smooth paste with flour, salt and remaining ¼ c cold milk. Add to hot milk and cook until mixture thickens. Heat vinegar and mustard together and add slowly to dressing. Fork whip egg with sugar and stir into dressing. Add butter. Pour over cabbage and serve hot or cold. 4 to 6 servings.

No one seems to know why this custard-filled, chocolate-iced yellow cake is called a pie, but try a **BOSTON CREAM PIE** *from a local bakery and you'll call it delicious.*

MICHIGAN — THE GREAT LAKES STATE

Capital	Lansing
Elevation	572 ft. to 1980 ft.
Population (1980)	9,109,000
(1990)	9,145,000
26th State	admitted Jan. 26, 1837
Tree	White Pine
Flower	Apple Blossom
Bird	Robin

WHILE IN MICHIGAN ...

CAMP along 3200 miles of shoreline, washed by four of the five Great Lakes. Sleeping Bear Dunes and Pictured Rocks are National Lakeshores.

EXPLORE the State Parks in summer, including Tahquamenon Falls, Porcupine Mountains and Hartwick Pines; revisit in winter for skiing or snowmobiling.

VISIT Thomas Edison's actual laboratory at Greenfield Village, where three centuries of history is condensed into a day's stroll.

CROSS three international bridges to Canada, visit Isle Royale National Park, or take a ferry to Mackinac Island and step into history.

WATCH 50,000 ton freighters being raised or lowered 21 feet between Lake Superior and Lake Huron at the Soo Locks.

TOUR factories — from the making of automobiles to corn flakes; red flannels to magic paraphernalia.

FISH in 11,000 inland lakes and 36,000 miles of rivers and streams as well as the Great Lakes for almost every variety of fish.

★ ★ ★ ★ ★ ★

WRITE for more information: Michigan Travel Bureau, P.O. Box 30226, Lansing, MI 48909.

TRY

GREAT LAKES DIP OR DINNER
or
CAMPERS' DELIGHT, see Ohio
or
CORNISH PASTIES, see Wisconsin
serve with
CARROT, CELERY, RAISIN SALAD
CHERRY CRISP or FRESH CHERRIES

Michigan produces about 75% of the nation's dry navy beans, according to our correspondent who shares this recipe from the Michigan Bean Commission.

GREAT LAKES DIP or DINNER

1 can (28 oz.) pork and beans
½ c cheddar cheese, shredded
1½ t garlic salt
  or ¼ t garlic powder
1 t chili powder
2 t vinegar
2 t Worcestershire sauce
½ t liquid smoke
4 slices bacon
salt, red pepper

Sieve, puree or mash beans. Heat in top of double boiler with rest of ingredients except salt and red pepper. When heated, add seasonings to taste. Top with bacon, fried until crisp; then crumbled. For an easy meal, serve hot over sliced ham or poached eggs on toast. As a dip, serve warm with corn chips or crackers.

★ Millicent Lane, Lansing, MI

Keilbasa, more commonly known as Polish sausage, was one of the many contributions to American cuisine by Polish immigrants, many of whom settled in communities around Detroit.

CAMPERS' DELIGHT, WITH POLISH SAUSAGE

Follow the recipe for Campers' Delight *(see Ohio)* by substituting 1 pound of Polish sausage for the pork sausage. Cut the sausage in four pieces, then slice each piece lengthwise. Place cut side down in a large frying pan and saute until brown. Remove and put vegetables into same pan; arrange sausages on top, cover and cook slowly until vegetables are done. To serve, place sausages on each plate, cut side up, and mound vegetables over them. 4 servings.

Although this recipe was shared by a Connecticut reader, cherries (both sweet and for pies) are so plentiful in Michigan, we took the liberty of transplanting:

CHERRY CRISP

1 can cherry pie filling
⅓ c flour
¾ c rolled oats
⅓ c sugar
⅓ c margarine

Place cherry pie filling in an 8x8-inch square baking dish. Combine flour, oats and sugar; cut in margarine until crumbly. Sprinkle evenly over cherry filling and bake at 350° for 30 minutes.

★ Hazel Bruyette, Hartford, CT

MINNESOTA — THE NORTH STAR STATE

Capital	Saint Paul
Elevation	602 ft. to 2301 ft.
Population (1980)	4,076,000
(1990)	4,214,000
32nd State	admitted May 11, 1858
Tree	Red Pine
Flower	Lady's Slipper
Bird	Loon

WHILE IN MINNESOTA...

CAMP at State Parks in any of Minnesota's four regions: Northeastern, North-central/West, Southern and Metro.

CHOOSE some of the countless marked hiking and snowmobile trails as they skirt many of the lakes and meander through forests.

WADE across the Mississippi at it's trickle-source in Itasca State Park; explore the French Voyageurs primitive region, or Paul Bunyan Country.

VISIT the famed Mayo clinic, Lindbergh's birthplace and Interpretive Center, Laura Ingalls Wilder's Walnut Grove, or "Old 201", Casey Jones' locomotive.

ATTEND Svenskarnes Dag, the major Swedish festival of the nation, the Hiawatha Pageant, a Renaissance Festival, or St. Paul's Winter Carnival.

WONDER at the Kensington Runestone — evidence of a Viking expedition in 1362 AD, or at Indian Rock carvings which may go back to 3000 BC.

FISH the clear lakes even in winter when 5,000 Ice Boats appear for dropping a line through holes cut in the ice.

★ ★ ★ ★ ★ ★

WRITE for more information: State of Minnesota, Tourism Division, 375 Jackson St., 250 Skyway Level, St. Paul, MN 55101.

TRY

SWEDISH MEATBALLS
or
BASS AND BANANAS
or
CAMPFIRE ROAST OR STEAK, see *Oklahoma*
serve with
CALICO POTATO SALAD
CELERY STICKS
FRESH BERRY "SHORTCAKES"

Swedes are synonomous with Minnesota, so start with:

SWEDISH MEATBALLS

1½ lb. ground beef	1/8 t *each* ginger & nutmeg
½ lb. ground pork	1 egg
1½ c soft bread crumbs	¼ c finely snipped
1 c light cream	parsley, or 1 T dry flakes
or 1 small can	1 c boiling water
evaporated milk	1 beef bouillon cube
½ c chopped onion	

In a large bowl, soak bread crumbs and cream or milk for five minutes. Add rest of ingredients, except water and bouillon cube. Chill mixture before shaping in 1-inch balls — wetting your hands helps keep the meat from sticking to them while you roll. Brown meatballs in skillet. Drain all but about 2 tablespoons fat. Dissolve bouillon cube in hot water and pour over meat. Cook slowly for 20 minutes. Remove meatballs to shallow serving bowl and keep warm while thickening liquid with 2 tablespoons flour stirred into ¼ cup cold water. Pour gravy over meatballs, tossing gently to coat well. 6 servings.

Also known as the "Land of 10,000 Lakes" (in reality there are over 15,000), Minnesota teems with fish. Bananas enhance the flavor of freshwater fish.

BANANAS AND BASS

Bass fillets
Bananas, ripe, but still firm — one per serving
Oil for frying

Cut bananas in half lengthwise and sizzle along with fish until both are brown. Takes only a few minutes per side.

CALICO POTATO SALAD

Add one grated carrot, a diced tomato, and a small can of drained peas to your favorite potato salad for a colorful, tasty touch.

FRESH BERRY "SHORTCAKES"

Buy a small poundcake loaf. Cut into ½-inch thick slices and cover with berries which have been sprinkled with sugar and allowed to sit until some juice is drawn out. Top with whipped topping, or pour rich cream over all.

MISSISSIPPI — THE MAGNOLIA STATE

Capital	Jackson
Altitude	sea level to 806 ft.
Population (1980)	2,520,638
(1990)	2,625,000
20th State	admitted Dec. 10, 1817
Tree	Magnolia
Flower	Magnolia
Bird	Mockingbird

WHILE IN MISSISSIPPI...

CAMP   in any of 24 State Parks — in forests, hills, plains, in the Mississippi Delta or on the Gulf Coast; or choose a Water Park.

STOP   first at a Welcome Center, a "mini-travel agency", with travel counselors, picnic facilities, restrooms, relaxing lounges and refreshments.

CRUISE   down the Mississippi on authentic sternwheelers, or float in a canoe down streams, rivers or creeks, past cypress swamps and lush farmlands.

FOLLOW   the Natchez Trace, and retrace overland journeys of Indian tribes, colonial travelers, the backwoods army of Andrew Jackson.

JOIN   a Pilgrimage to antebellum mansions set among stately magnolias; visit a working plantation, or a quaint township.

CATCH   the surf at Gulf Islands National Seashore, or take the kids to a Wave Pool where high speed fans create wave action.

FISH   in rivers, streams, lakes, reservoirs and bayous for bass, crappie, catfish, gar and more. Gulf of Mexico waters yield a great variety — from bluefish, flounder, pompano, sea trout to whiting.

★ ★ ★ ★ ★ ★ ★

WRITE   for more information: Division of Tourism, P.O. Box 22825, Jackson, MS 39205.

TRY

AUNT JENNY'S CATFISH
or
SHRIMP GUMBO
or
CHICKEN WITH SOUTHERN BARBECUE SAUCE, see *Alabama*
serve with
HOT BUTTERED RICE
JOHNNYCAKE
CARROT AND CELERY STICKS
FRESH OR CANNED SLICED PEACHES

Think Mississippi and think catfish! An avid RV-er shares this delicious preparation method, adapted from an Ocean Springs' restaurant recipe.

AUNT JENNY'S CATFISH

2 lb. catfish fillets	2 T flour
¼ c cornmeal	pepper, to taste
2 T flour	2 T water
	oil for frying*

Combine all ingredients except catfish and oil in a shallow bowl. Roll fish in batter, then deep fry until brown. (May also be fried in ¼ inch of fat, turning carefully to brown both sides.) 4 servings.

*Peanut oil is best, but any light cooking oil may be used.

★ Kathy Rhodes, New Castle, CA

You may not be able to attend the picturesque "Blessing of the Shrimp Fleet", but you can salute the state's seafood industry with:

SHRIMP GUMBO

2 slices bacon	¼ t thyme leaves
1 med. onion, chopped	1/8 t hot pepper sauce
1 green pepper, chunked	½ c okra, sliced
1 garlic clove, minced	salt and pepper, to taste
1 can (16 oz.) tomatoes	½ lb. shrimp

Fry bacon in a large saucepan until partially cooked. Add onions, bell pepper and garlic; saute until bacon is crisp. Stir in undrained tomatoes, breaking into small pieces with a spoon. Add remaining ingredients except shrimp. Simmer gently, uncovered, until thickened and vegetables are cooked, about 20 minutes. Add shrimp, if fresh — cook only until pink; if cooked, just until heated through. 4 servings.

Hot breads are a traditional favorite of Mississippians for almost every meal. One of the earliest is Johnnycake, first called "Journey Cakes" because they were carried in large batches by travelers into the wilderness. Originally made only with stone-ground white cornmeal, boiling water and salt and fried in bacon grease, this enriched version gradually evolved in the South.

JOHNNYCAKES

2 eggs	2 T shortening, melted
1 c water	½ t salt
¾ c milk	2 c yellow cornmeal

Beat eggs in a medium-sized bowl. Stir in water, milk, shortening and salt. Gradually add cornmeal, mixing well. Stir batter before making each cake. Pour a scant ¼ cup batter on a hot, well-greased griddle, spreading to ¼ inch thick. Cook 3 to 4 minutes on each side, until golden brown. Serve warm with butter, and maple syrup if desired. 12 to 14 johnnycakes.

MISSOURI — THE "SHOW ME" STATE

Capital	Jefferson City
Elevation	230 ft. to 1772 ft.
Population (1980)	4,917,000
(1990)	5,066,000
24th State	admitted Aug. 10, 1821
Tree	Dogwood
Flower	Hawthorn
Bird	Bluebird

WHILE IN MISSOURI ...

CAMP in most of the 46 State Parks and 28 State Historic Sites. Elephant Rocks State Park (over a billion years old) provides a Braille Trail.

IMAGINE how prehistoric mastadons, outlaws, and even beer garden patrons felt in some of the state's 5000 caves — 24 open for tours.

RELIVE the days of Mark Twain at Hannibal on the Mississippi, at his Boyhood Home; Mark Twain Cave, Lake, and Museum.

ENTER the "Gateway to the West" — the St. Louis Arch with elevators to the top and the Museum of Westward Expansion below.

VISIT the focal point of 19th century steamboat, freight and stage lines, St. Joseph, where the Pony Express began its historic venture.

WANDER through an elegant 1920's plaza, Heritage Village, Missouri Town 1855; or frolic at one of the world's largest aquatic parks — all in or near Kansas City.

FLOAT a placid stream in a canoe or john boat in the Ozark National Scenic Riverways. Fish a little along the quiet way.

★ ★ ★ ★ ★ ★

WRITE for more information: Division of Tourism, Box 1055, Jefferson City, MO 65102.

TRY

FISHERMAN'S STEW
or
HAMBURGERS
or
CHICKEN CORN SOUP, see Pennsylvania
serve with
GREEN BEAN AND ONION SALAD, see Delaware
FRENCH FRIES
COFFEE CAN ICE CREAM

Reputed to have more miles of fishing streams and rivers than any other state, Missouri is a fisherman's paradise. Perhaps you've caught so many, you're tired of fried, so try:

FISHERMAN'S STEW

½ lb. cleaned, boned fish	1 c water
4 small potatoes	¼ c white wine
2 medim onions	salt and pepper
¼ c oil	1 (16 oz.) can peas
1 (10½ oz.) can cream	& carrots, drained
of mushroom soup	1 c cherry tomatoes

Cut fish into bite-size pieces and set aside. Slice potatoes and onion into thin slices; cook until lightly browned in hot oil. Stir in soup, water and seasonings. Bring to boil; simmer 5 minutes. Add fish and vegetables; simmer until fish flakes easily, about 6-8 minutes. Add tomatoes and heat through. Serve with lemon wedges. 4 servings.

★ L. Thomas, Fox Island, WA

Tradition says that the Hamburger as well as the ice cream cone was introduced first at the St. Louis World's Fair of 1904. Since most every cook has their own favorite way of fixing hamburgers, we won't go into that. However, the idea of homemade ice-cream on a camping trip is so intriguing, we'd like to share:

COFFEE CAN ICE CREAM

You will need a 3 pound and a 1 pound coffee can, each with a plastic lid; 20 cups (about 8 pounds) crushed ice; 1½ cups rock salt. Into the 1 pound can pour:

1 c whipping cream	1 egg, well beaten
1 c milk	¾ c finely chopped
½ c sugar	fruit - peaches, cherries
1 t vanilla	pineapple, berries

Cover, and place in the center of the large can. Fill the empty space between cans with alternating layers of ONE-HALF of the ice and salt. Place plastic lid securely on the large can.

Find a nice, level spot and seat two volunteers about three feet apart. Have them roll the can back and forth between them for 10 minutes.

Remove the smaller can, rinsing free of salt and ice. Dry the lid, remove, and scrape the frozen ice-cream from the sides into the middle. Empty the large can; repack with remaining ice and salt. Repeat the rolling process for 5 more minutes. Scrape down as before. Serve in small cones. 5 ½ cup servings.

MONTANA — THE TREASURE STATE

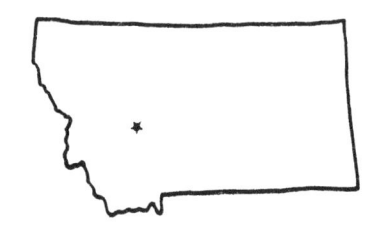

Capital	Helena
Elevation	1800 ft to 12,799 ft.
Population (1980)	801,000
(1990)	819,000
41st State	admitted Nov. 8, 1889
Flower	Bitterroot
Bird	Meadowlark
Tree	Ponderosa Pine

WHILE IN MONTANA...

CAMP   in your choice of 10 State Parks, 2 National or nearly 500 developed campsite areas, maintained by other State and National agencies.

REACH   one Lewis and Clark quest, where the Jefferson, Madison and Gallatin Rivers join to form the headwaters of the Mighty Missouri.

CLAMP   on the "skinny skis" for cross-country; snowmobile marked and scenic trails; ice fish; enjoy every imaginable winter activity.

CROSS   the Continental Divide in Glacier National Park while you marvel at its 50 glaciers; include Flathead Lake for fantastic fishing.

SEE   the Home/Museum of Charles M. Russell, famous Western artist; also the Great Falls High School transformed to an arts and shopping complex.

VIEW   unusual badlands that resemble a moonscape at Makoshika and the site of the Sioux and Cheyenne defeat of Custer.

TOP   it all with a stay at Yellowstone — the nation's oldest park, renowned for brilliant pools, mud pots, spouting geysers, especially "Old Faithful".

★ ★ ★ ★ ★ ★ ★

WRITE   for more information: State Board of Tourism, Dept. of Commerce, Helena, MT 59620.

TRY

PAN BROILED BUFFALO STEAKS
or
WHOLE TROUT COOKED IN FOIL, *see Colorado*
or
CALICO BEANS, *see Wyoming*
serve with
SUNSHINE SALAD
CORN ON THE COB
GATEWAY GINGERBREAD

As the pioneers pushed their way westward, the noon stop was brief. If they had been lucky enough to shoot a buffalo, the more tender cuts were saved for "nooning" so they could be pan-broiled over a quick fire. You can find buffalo meat in Montana markets and sample:

PAN BROILED BUFFALO

Heat skillet to high temperature. Sprinkle salt generously over the bottom of the pan. Put buffalo steak in the pan and when the blood just begins to show on the top side, turn and brown other side. Cook until done to your taste.

Montanans are reputed to have a high regard for carrots, even turning them into "pumpkin" pies. However, they are never better than in:

SUNSHINE SALAD

1 pkg. lemon gelatin
1 c grated carrot
1 c grated cabbage
½ c celery, chopped
1 (8 oz.) can crushed pineapple
mayonnaise
lettuce

Mix gelatin according to package directions and chill until slightly thickened. Combine rest of ingredients except lettuce; stir into gelatin. Pour into a 9x11 inch pan and chill until set. Cut into squares and serve on lettuce leaves. 6 servings.

Montana claims a small strip of Yellowstone National Park, with a spectacular entrance through the Rockies. A good "journey cake" to take when you visit the Geysers and Mud Pots is this sturdy:

GATEWAY GINGERBREAD

2 eggs
¼ c sugar
½ c light molasses
1 c sour cream*
1½ c flour
1 t soda
½ t salt
2 t ginger

Beat eggs; add sugar and molasses and continue beating until well blended. Beat in sour cream. Mix and sift dry ingredients and add to egg mixture, beating until smooth. Bake in an 8x8 inch greased and floured baking dish for 30 minutes at 350° or until top springs back when lightly touched. 6 servngs.

*Can use 1 (8 oz.) can evaporated milk blended with 1 tablespoon vinegar.

NEBRASKA — THE CORNHUSKER STATE

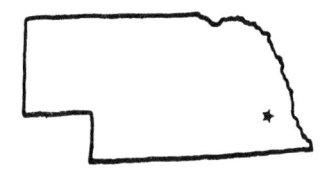

Capital	Lincoln
Elevation	840 ft. to 5,426 ft.
Population (1980)	1,586,000
(1990)	1,598,000
37th State	admitted March 1, 1867
Tree	Cottonwood
Flower	Goldenrod
Bird	Western Meadowlark

WHILE IN NEBRASKA ...

CAMP — in any of 86 State and Federal Camping Areas, all within easy access of major highways.

FOLLOW — the Oregon, California and Mormon Trails; the Pony Express and Overland Stage Routes on the Great Platte River Road (now I-80).

WANDER — leisurely through the Old Market featuring "turn-of-the-century" brick streets, special entertainment, craft fairs and quaint shops.

CHOOSE — a Festival — Arbor Day, Hay Market, Country Music, Threshing Bee, Cornhusking; or Danish, Swedish, German, Czech, Grecian, La Fiesta Italiana.

SAMPLE — Native American foods and entertainments with the Winnebago, Santee or Omaha tribes as they celebrate their summer Pow-Wows.

SWIM — and fish, water ski or canoe, do some ice fishing in the state's many lakes, huge reservoirs, rivers and streams.

MOTOR — with assurance that beautiful roadside Visitor's Centers and highway signs with Radio Stations' frequencies will give you needed information.

★ ★ ★ ★ ★ ★

WRITE — for more information: Division of Travel and Tourism, Box 94666, Lincoln, NE 68509.

TRY

HOMINY HARMONY
or
GRILLED REUBEN
or
GRILLED LEMON CHICKEN *see Colorado*
serve with
TOSSED GREEN SALAD
BARBECUED CORN IN THE HUSKS
SPICY APPLESAUCE *see Colorado*

Corn was such an available staple to early pioneers, that 33 different recipes using corn were listed in a Nebraska farm paper of 1862.

HOMINY HARMONY

1 lb. ground beef	1 (10½) oz. can tomato
1 med. onion	soup
1 large bell pepper	1 (16 oz.) can hominy
½ lb. cheddar cheese	salt and pepper

Crumble ground beef in a large frying pan. Cook slowly until most fat is released, then pour off all but two tablespoons fat. Add sliced onion and bell pepper cut into strips. Stir in undiluted tomato soup and drained hominy; cook slowly until heated through. Sprinkle with shredded cheese. Cover and heat until cheese melts. 6 servings.

"The Reuben" was the winner of a 1956 National Sandwich Idea Contest, submitted by a restaurant cook from Omaha.

GRILLED REUBEN

8 large slices rye bread	½ c well-drained
•6 T Thousand Island dressing	sauerkraut
4 slices Swiss cheese	sliced cooked or canned
softened butter or margarine	corned beef

Spread dressing on 4 slices of bread. Cover with cheese, 2 tablespoons sauerkraut, and several very thin slices of corned beef. (Canned corned beef slices more easily when chilled.) Top with second slice of bread. Spread butter on tops and bottoms of sandwiches. Grill on both sides in skillet over medium heat until cheese melts. 4 sandwiches.

What better place than in the cornhusker state to fix:

BARBECUED CORN IN THE HUSKS

fresh corn on the cob   butter or margarine

Pick out fresh corn, with the cobs uncut and the husks intact. Strip off tough outer husks and tear several into ¼-inch ties for later use. Pull down the tender inside husks, being careful to leave attached, and remove silk. Brush kernels with about 2 teaspoons butter per ear. Pull up the husks, covering the corn completely. Tie with reserved corn husk strips. Soak ears in cold water for 20 to 30 minutes. Remove from water, drain, and place on grill about 6 inches above hot coals. Turn every 3 or 4 minutes and cook until dark golden, about 15 to 20 minutes total.

NEVADA — THE SILVER STATE

Capital	Carson City
Elevation	479 ft. to 13,140 ft.
Population (1980)	881,000
(1990)	963,000
36th State	admitted Oct. 31, 1864
Trees	Bristlecone Pine
	Single-leaf pinon
Flower	Sagebrush
Bird	Mountain bluebird

WHILE IN NEVADA...

CAMP   at Lake Tahoe, Lake Mead, on the Colorado River, or in your choice of 21 State parks throughout the state.

CATCH   Nevada-type action at its glittering cities, or head for the great out of doors — Valley of Fire or Red Rock Canyon.

MARVEL   at the most complete collection of antique and celebrity cars in history; cheer Chariot Races; catch Indian Pow Wows and Rodeos.

VISIT   Virginia City and the Comstock, once a thriving silver mining area — remembered for Mark Twain — and which still holds Camel Races.

TAKE   the elevator descent of approximately 70 stories to the interior base of Hoover (Boulder) Dam holding the Colorado River at Lake Mead.

SKI   at Mt. Charleston in Southern Nevada or at internationally-famous Tahoe with nineteen full-service resorts in the mountains encircling the lake.

FISH   with confidence for stripers and largemouth bass at Lake Mead, walleye or cutthroat at Tahoe and Pyramid, and in several large reservoirs.

★ ★ ★ ★ ★ ★ ★

WRITE   for more information: Nevada Dept. of Tourism, Capitol Complex, Carson City, NV 89710. Or call 1-800-237-0774.

TRY

QUICK PORCUPINE MEATBALLS
or
DORIS' SURPRISE PACKAGE, *see Alaska*
or
GRILLED LAMB CHOPS, *see Wyoming*
serve with
SHEEPHERDER'S POTATOES
MIXED GREEN SALAD
ROCKY ROAD COOKIES

Born during the Depression to help stretch meat budgets, this has become popular for camping and can be a one-dish meal by adding a can of drained green beans the last few minutes of cooking.

QUICK PORCUPINE MEATBALLS

1 lb. ground beef	1 T oil
½ t salt	¼ c chopped onion
dash of pepper	½ c catsup
⅔ c instant rice	½ c water

Mix together beef, salt, pepper and INSTANT rice. Form into about 16 balls. Brown meatballs and onions in heated oil. Mix catsup and water, pour over meatballs. Cover and simmer about 20 to 30 minutes. 4 servings.

Sheepherding Basques added their simple, hearty fare to Nevada cookery.

SHEEPHERDER'S POTATOES

4-6 strips bacon	salt and pepper
4 large potatoes	½ c water

Cut bacon into one inch slices. Brown in medium skillet and remove. Drain all but 2 Tablespoons fat. Pare potatoes and slice thinly (or scrub well and leave on the skins). Add to hot bacon fat; season to taste. Add water and cover, stirring occasionally until most potato slices are brown. Remove cover for last 10 minutes; add bacon and heat through.

The owner of a Reno restaurant developed Rocky Road Ice Cream — originally made with chocolate marshmallows and nuts added to vanilla ice cream. Our "Road" omits the ice cream but keeps the "Rocks" and rich chocolate flavor.

ROCKY ROAD COOKIES

¼ lb. milk chocolate bar	½ c nuts, coarsely chopped
1 c miniature marshmallows	16 Graham crackers

In a double boiler, melt chocolate; remove from heat and stir in marshmallows and nuts. Spread thickly on 8 graham cracker squares, top with remaining squares. Allow to cool until chocolate hardens. 8 cookies.

NEW HAMPSHIRE — THE GRANITE STATE

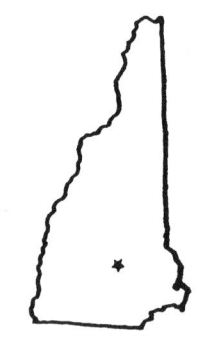

Capital	Concord
Elevation	sea level to 6288 ft.
Population (1980)	951,000
(1990)	1,027,000
9th state	admitted June 21, 1788
Tree	Birch
Flower	Purple Lilac
Bird	Purple Finch

WHILE IN NEW HAMPSHIRE...

CAMP   in White Mountain National Forest containing Mt. Washington, at 6,288 feet, the highest mountain in New England.

ENJOY   the cool summers in many State Parks, noted mainly for their recreational facilities.

RIDE   the aerial tramway at Franconia Notch, which provides spectacular views of the narrow river gorge.

FISH   in mountain streams, ponds, larger rivers and lakes; and along New Hampshire's 18 miles of shoreline.

SKI   in over 50 ski areas. Mt. Washington also provides ice-climbing above the timberline.

TOUR   the home, studios and gardens of American sculptor Augustus Saint-Gaudens at the National Historic Site bearing his name.

VISIT   New Hampshire's statewide history museum in Concord, the Robert Frost homestead in Derry, or the Christa McCauliffe Planetarium, also in Concord.

★ ★ ★ ★ ★ ★

WRITE   for more information: Dept. of Resources and Economic Development, Office of Vacation Travel, P.O. Box 856, Concord, NH 03301.

TRY

PAN-FRIED SCROD
or
CORNED BEEF & CABBAGE
or
BRAISED CHICKEN, *see Rhode Island*
BOILED POTATOES
YANKEE SLAW, *see Massachusetts*
BLUEBERRY SLUMP

Scrod is baby cod, a favorite of New Englanders.

PAN-FRIED SCROD

8 T butter or margarine	½ t grated nutmeg
1 lb. Scrod fillets, cut into large pieces	1 T lemon juice
	1 T chopped parsley (optional)
Salt, pepper to taste	

Melt 4 tablespoons butter in large frying pan. Add the fish fillets, and fry on low heat 4 to 6 minutes, turning occasionally, until fish flakes easily. Keep fish warm while making the sauce: Add remaining butter, seasonings and lemon juice to the pan and simmer until butter is melted. Pour over fish. 4 servings.

The Scotch-Irish immigrants who introduced the potato to New Hampshire in about 1720 also brought their version of the New England boiled dinner.

CORNED BEEF and CABBAGE

2 cans (12 oz. ea.) corned beef	¾ c milk
1 head cabbage	¼ t pepper

Chill corned beef (for easier slicing), then cut into 6 pieces. Cut cabbage into 6 wedges. Place corned beef portions and a wedge of cabbage on 14-inch squares of heavy duty aluminum foil. Dribble 2 tablespoons of milk between the cabbage leaves in each portion. Seal foil and place over medium heat — above coals, in a frying pan or in the oven for 30 minutes. Turn packets once. 4-6 servings.

Fruit desserts with the odd names of slumps, grunts and flummeries were all true products of New England cooking.

BLUEBERRY SLUMP

1 lb. fresh blueberries	2½ T lemon juice
¼ c sugar	¼ c maple syrup
1 t allspice	1 c biscuit mix

Combine the sauce ingredients in medium saucepan. Warm over low heat, stirring constantly until sugar is dissolved. Continue cooking and stirring for 5 more minutes. Keep warm while mixing biscuit topping from 1 cup biscuit mix, (prepared according to package directions), enriched with 2 T oil. Drop dough by tablespoon over the sauce until blueberry mixture is completely covered. Cover and simmer for 20 minutes, or until topping is puffed and dry. 4 servings.

NEW JERSEY — THE GARDEN STATE

Capital	Trenton
Elevation	sea level to 1803 ft.
Population (1980)	7,438,000
(1990)	7,619,000
3rd State	admitted Dec. 18, 1787
Tree	Red Oak
Flower	Violet
Bird	Goldfinch

WHILE IN NEW JERSEY...

CAMP in Washington Crossing State Park, near the Delaware Water Gap, or on the Southern Shores where more than 25,000 campsites await you.

FIND the wilderness sanctuary for wild flowers, even orchids, that bloom nowhere else on earth; or gasp at the incredible expanse of cranberry bogs.

SEE historic Wheaton Village, or Waterloo Village where craftspeople keep Colonial days alive, or Speedwell Village, preserving 19th century life-styles.

VISIT The Edison National Historic Site and Museum in West Orange where he invented and patented over 500 items.

TAKE a ferry through the busy harbor for a thrilling ride from Liberty State Park to the Statue of Liberty or Ellis Island.

STROLL along the fabled 6-mile Boardwalk in Atlantic City. Enjoy Ocean One Pier, a casino, the tram or other boardwalks along the Southern Beaches.

FISH in 1400 miles of trout streams for trout, black bass, crappie ... or try for saltwater species including sea trout, kingfish, bluefin tuna.

★ ★ ★ ★ ★ ★

WRITE for more information: Division of Travel & Tourism, C.N. 826, Trenton, NJ 08625 or call for literature: 1-800-JERSEY-7.

TRY

CAMPERS' CLAM SPAGHETTI
or
MONSTER SALAD
or
CINCINNATI PORK CHOPS, *see Ohio*
serve with
HOT GARLIC BREAD or CRUSTY ROLLS
SUCCOTASH
SWAMP HUCKLEBERRY PUDDING

Italian immigrants, settling on the New Jersey shore, brought along their fondness for spaghetti, and when they dressed it with a clam sauce, this dish became typically American.

That it has spread to the West Coast is verified by our contributor who says she has "made it with dried materials camping at Lake Powell, and in a trailer with fresh materials in the Northwest."

CAMPERS' CLAM SPAGHETTI

2 T oil (or bacon grease saved from breakfast)
1 med. onion minced (or 2 T dry minced onion)
½ c chopped parsley (or 2 T dry minced)
1 can baby clams, or 2 (6 oz.) cans minced clams
½ c white wine or extra clam juice
2-4 cloves garlic, minced (or ½ t dry minced)
Spaghetti for 2

Heat oil or bacon grease in skillet. Add onion, parsley and garlic. (If fresh, lightly saute — do not burn garlic). Add clams and extra liquid and simmer down (about 10 min.). May be thickened with a little flour or cornstarch mixed in water. Serve over hot spaghetti.

★ Halcyon H. Winter, San Jose, CA

A New Jerseyite shares a recipe that she says "makes you wonder if someone has raided a Garden State garden!"

MONSTER SALAD

Start with: 1 head lettuce, 2 carrots, 2 tomatoes, 2 ribs celery.

Slice everything onto a large platter. Add anything else on hand — broccoli, cauliflower, green onions, radishes, zucchini ... For a full meal, include shredded cheese and sliced cold cuts or strips of chicken, ham or turkey. Drizzle on a little oil. Add a moderate splash of wine vinegar (garlic flavored is "GREAT"). Salt and pepper to taste.

★ Ronda Wisniewski, S. Plainfield, NJ

Adopted from the Indians by early settlers, nearly every state has its own version of:

SUCCOTASH

1 can lima beans   ½ c cream or
1 can whole kernel corn   evaporated milk
pepper   2 T butter or margarine

Drain, and stir together the beans and corn. Add milk or cream. Heat just to boiling. Add butter, sprinkle with pepper. 4 servings.

Long before Columbus arrived, the Indians picked blueberries in Whitesbog in the Pine Barrens of New Jersey. The white settlers called them Swamp Huckleberries.

SWAMP HUCKLEBERRY PUDDING

To make this pudding, simply stir in one or two cups of fresh blueberries just before serving instant vanilla pudding.

NEW MEXICO — LAND OF ENCHANTMENT

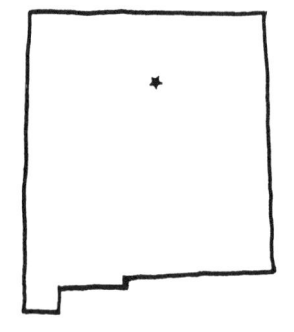

Capital	Santa Fe
Elevation	2,817 ft. to 13,161 ft.
Population (1980)	1,359,000
(1990)	1,479,000
47th State	admitted Jan. 6, 1912
Tree	Pinon
Flower	Yucca
Bird	Roadrunner

WHILE IN NEW MEXICO ...

EXPLORE six national forests, ranging from a cacti-splotched desert to fir-covered mountains, where over 200 campgrounds are available.

MARVEL at Carlsbad Caverns, a National Park and the largest known underground labyrinth in the world.

CATCH an Indian celebration or Arts and Crafts Fair. There are 19 Pueblo, 4 Navajo and 2 Apache reservations in New Mexico.

BROWSE through art galleries in Taos, founded in 1617, and an artist colony since 1898. Kit Carson's last home is here.

SKI in 14 ski areas, including Red River with a 1524 foot drop; and Sandia whose tramway at 2.7 miles is the longest in the world.

TRAVEL in time from per-historic cliff-dwellings, through ghost towns of the Wild West, to the International Space Hall of Fame.

FISH in many man-made lakes and major rivers, including the Rio Grande, for 4 species of trout, bass, pike, walleye, crappie, kokonee.

★ ★ ★ ★ ★ ★

WRITE for more information: New Mexico Tourism & Travel Division, Bataan Memorial Building, Room 101, Santa Fe, NM 87503.

TRY

STACKED ENCHILADAS
or
POSOLE
or
DOROTHY'S TEXAS CHILI, *see Texas*
serve with
SPANISH SETTLERS' RICE
COOL-DOWN SALAD, *see Arizona*
CACTUS CANDY, *from a local store*

Authentic New Mexican enchiladas are stacked, not rolled.
STACKED ENCHILADAS

½ c onion, finely chopped
2 T lard (or oil)
1 T flour
1 (4 oz.) can green chili peppers, chopped
½ t salt
1 lb. ground beef crumbled and cooked
1 (8 oz.) can tomatoes
8 corn tortillas, ¼ c oil
1 c Monterey Jack cheese, shredded

In a large skillet, cook onion in lard until limp. Stir in flour; add milk, peppers and salt. Cook over low heat, stirring constantly until thick. Add beef and tomatoes and heat through. Heat tortillas (one at a time) until limp in oil heated in a small skillet, about 15 seconds per side. Drain on paper towels. Place a tortilla in a 9x9-inch baking pan, cover with about ¼ cup beef mixture and sprinkle with cheese. Repeat until the stack is complete, then bake in a 350° oven for 20 minutes. Remove two tortillas for each serving. 4 servings.

Traditionally made with the scraps of meat left at hog-butchering time, this dish is named for the type of hominy used.
POSOLE

1½ lb. boneless pork, cubed
1½ c water
1 t salt
2 (14½ oz.) cans hominy
¼ c onion, chopped
1 clove garlic, minced
½ t cumin
¼ t oregano
bottled red chili sauce

Cut fat from the pork and cook in a heavy skillet until about 2 tablespoons of drippings are released. Remove trimmings, add pork and cook until brown. Stir in water and salt. Cover and simmer about 30 minutes until pork is cooked and tender. Add undrained hominy and rest of ingredients. Simmer, covered, for 15 minutes. Serve with chili sauce.

Early Spanish settlers prepared their rice with fresh herbs, rather than chilis.
SPANISH SETTLERS' RICE

1 T oil
½ c green pepper, chopped
¼ c onion, chopped
½ - 1 t garlic salt
½ t dried basil, crushed
½ t dried rosemary
2 c water
1 c rice
salt and pepper to taste
1 tomato, chopped

Heat oil in a heavy saucepan. Add pepper, onion and first three seasonings; cook until tender. Add water and bring to boiling, then stir in rice. Turn heat to medium-low. Cover and simmer about 15 minutes until rice is done and all liquid is absorbed. Add salt and pepper as needed. Stir in tomato, stirring until heated through. 6 servings.

NEW YORK — THE EMPIRE STATE

Capital	Albany
Elevation	sea level to 5344 ft.
Population (1980)	17,659,000
(1990)	17,772,000
11th State	admitted July 26, 1788
Tree	Sugar Maple
Flower	Rose
Bird	Bluebird

WHILE IN NEW YORK...

CAMP   in any of over 500 public and private campgrounds; RV sites in 66 State Parks. For reservations at all State Parks, call 1-800-456-CAMP.

VISIT   the cavern where 150 subterranean weddings have been performed; then to Niagara — "Wonder of the World" for happy honeymooners.

CATCH   your breath on a Hudson Cruise at the beauty of the majestic Palisades, the Taconic mountains, West Point, and the Catskills.

RENT   a houseboat and sail among the Thousand Islands in the St. Lawrence Seaway for total rest and relaxation.

CHOOSE   your pleasure from: The Finger Lakes, Leatherstocking, Adirondacks, Long Island, Chautauqua, Capital-Saratoga Regions.

SKI   the finest facilities in over 50 sites — half equipped for night skiing and one the location of former Winter Olympics.

TAKE   a bite of "The Big Apple" — New York City: Statue of Liberty, Greenwich Village, Broadway, U.N., Harbor Cruise, Rockefeller Center, Rockettes, Trade Center. More!

★ ★ ★ ★ ★ ★

WRITE   for more information: New York State Dept. of Economic Development, One Commerce Plaza, Albany, NY 12245.

TRY

MANHATTAN CLAM CHOWDER
or
PASTA E FAGIOLI
or
PORK POT PIE, see *Pennsylvania*
serve with
TOSSED GREEN SALAD
CELERY STICKS
HOT BUTTERED ROLLS
GRAPES WITH SOUR CREAM

Once you leave the New England States, clam chowder turns pink. New Yorkers disdain the pale variety, and tomatoes always appear in:

MANHATTAN CLAM CHOWDER

¼ c salt pork or bacon
¼ c minced onion
2 (7½ oz.) cans minced clams
2 c finely diced raw potatoes
1 stalk celery, diced
1 c water

1 (16 oz.) can tomatoes
¼ t thyme, optional
2 t minced parsley
  or ½ t parsley flakes
1 t salt
1/8 t pepper

In a large saucepan, fry finely cut pork or bacon with onion; pour off all but about 2 tablespoons fat. Drain minced clam liquid into pan, add potatoes, celery and water. Cook about 10 minutes, until potatoes are tender. Stir in tomatoes and seasonings. Bring to a boil, then add clams and bring just to a simmer. Serve immediately. Especially good with Pilot Crackers. 4-6 servings.

Meat was a luxury to early Italian immigrants, so beans were added to Pasta dishes for extra protein.

PASTA E FAGIOLI
(mispronounced "Pasta Fazool")

1 can kidney beans (15 oz.)
1 (8 oz.) can tomatoes
1 (8 oz.) can tomato sauce
1 med. carrot, chopped
½ small onion, chopped
1 c chopped celery

1 clove garlic, minced
salt and pepper to taste
1 T olive oil (optional)
1 c dry macaroni, cooked
  until tender
Grated Parmesan cheese

In a large saucepan, combine undrained beans and tomatoes; add rest of ingredients except macaroni, oil, and cheese. Cover and simmer for about 30 minutes. Add oil, then stir in cooked macaroni. Sprinkle with Parmesan. 4 servings.

The Finger Lakes region is famous for its grapes and wine. Pick up a bunch of green seedless grapes and treat yourself to:

GRAPES WITH SOUR CREAM

4 c green seedless grapes
¾ c sour cream
⅓ c brown sugar (dark preferred)

Wash, dry and chill stemmed grapes. Toss gently in a serving bowl with sour cream; sprinkle with sugar. (Best made at serving time.)

NORTH CAROLINA — THE TAR HEEL STATE

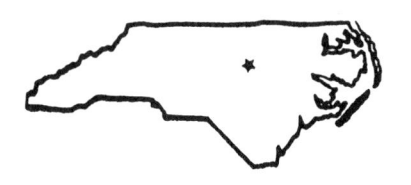

Capital	Raleigh
Altitude	sea level to 6684 ft.
Population (1980)	6,019,000
(1990)	6,333,000
12th State	admitted Nov. 21, 1789
Tree	Pine
Flower	Dogwood
Bird	Cardinal

WHILE IN NORTH CAROLINA...

CAMP in State Parks, from the Appalachian and Great Smoky Mountains to sunny beaches, or in National Forests and Seashores.

THRILL to America's oldest outdoor drama, "The Lost Colony" which re-enacts the first English attempt to settle America 400 years ago.

STEP into the past at Historic Bath and Historic Halifax, at the State Government Complex, at Wright Brothers National Memorial.

DRIVE along the Blue Ridge Parkway to admire rhododendrons, the Daniel Boone native gardens, Oconaluftee Indian Village, Linville caverns.

ATTEND a Festival — from Apple to Pumpkin, Colonial Craft to Curing Barn, Clog to Square Dance, even Hollerin' and Whistlin'.

DISCOVER Whitewater Falls whose 411-foot upper cascade is the highest in Eastern U.S. or take a ferry to the tallest lighthouse in America.

TOUR a textile mill, a peanut plantation, a furniture factory.

★ ★ ★ ★ ★ ★

WRITE for more information: State Board of Tourism, 430 N. Salisbury St., Raleigh, NC 27603.

TRY

CIDER-BRAISED HAM
with sweet potatoes
or
EASY SOUTHERN-FRIED CHICKEN
with rice
or
POTATO-SHRIMP SALAD, see *Florida*
serve with:
CANNED GREEN BEANS
APPLESAUCE AND COOKIES

If you happen to be in North Carolina in October, you can watch the making of apple cider. However, you can enjoy this recipe any time of the year.

CIDER-BRAISED HAM

1½ lb. ham steak or slices of canned ham	2 T flour
	2 c apple cider
2 T oil for browning	Powdered cloves

Brown ham slices in oil. Stir flour in ¼ cup cider. Pour remainder over ham and slowly stir in cider and flour mixture. Cook slowly for 20 minutes. Turn ham slice once. Dust lightly with cloves. 4-6 servings.

Opinions differ in the South as to the "proper" method of preparing the chicken before frying. Here's one of the simplest.

EASY SOUTHEN-FRIED CHICKEN

3 lbs. fryer pieces	Salt and pepper
1 c flour	Oil for frying

Pat chicken pieces dry. Mix flour and seasonings in a paper bag. Add a few chicken pieces at a time and shake to coat well. Heat ½ inch of oil in a heavy frying pan. Start with the meaty pieces, turn to brown evenly (about 5 to 10 minutes). Push aside, and add rest of chicken, browning well.

Cover skillet; turn heat to low and cook 10 minutes, then turn and cook, covered, another 10 minutes. Remove cover, increase heat and cook 5 to 10 minutes to re-crisp chicken.

Whatever method you use for cooking chicken, almost all Southerners agree on the merits of gravy, poured over the chicken and/or on biscuits, cornbread, potatoes or rice.

CREAM GRAVY

2 T fat from cooking chicken	
2 T flour	Salt and pepper
1 c milk	Dash of nutmeg

Pour off all but 2 tablespoons fat from pan in which chicken has been cooked. Add flour, then cook for 2 or 3 minutes, stirring constantly. Take pan off heat while you add the milk — to avoid lumps. Return pan to heat, stirring and scraping bottom to incorporate all the brown bits. Boil aboil 3 or 4 minutes. Season and serve.

NOTE: If you have a covered jar handy, you can put in the milk, flour and seasonings, then shake well and stir slowly into the chicken fat, cooking as above.

NORTH DAKOTA — THE SIOUX STATE

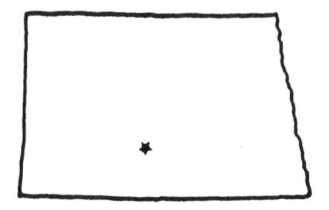

Capital	Bismarck
Elevation	750 ft. to 3,506 ft.
Population (1980)	670,000
(1990)	679,000
39th state	admitted Nov. 2, 1889
Tree	Elm
Flower	Wild Prairie Rose
Bird	Meadowlark

WHILE IN NORTH DAKOTA ...

CAMP   at any of 16 State Parks. Most are water-oriented — on lakes, rivers or streams, and many feature horse trails.

EXPLORE   Theodore Roosevelt National Park in the wildly scenic badlands where buffalo, deer and antelope roam, and prairie dogs guard their "towns".

VISIT   restored pioneer cattle towns, with exhibits, festivals, zoos, museums. Wander through the Custer House, Indian Villages and Fur Trade sites.

FISH   in lakes, rivers or reservoirs for walleye and northern pike, among many other varieties of native fish. Trout and salmon have been stocked.

WANDER   through the natural and landscaped beauty of International Peace Gardens on the Canadian border, and admire towers, chapels, pavilions.

TOUR   the North Dakota Heritage Center with one of the finest collections of Plains Indians artifacts in the world.

SKI   cross-country in most State Parks, and down-hill at resorts. Or try ice-fishing or snowmobiling.

★ ★ ★ ★ ★ ★

WRITE   for more information: North Dakota Tourism, 604 East Boulevard, Bismarck, ND 58505.

TRY

SIMPLE CHICKEN FRICASEE
or
WIENERS AND SAUERKRAUT
or
DENVER SANDWICH, *see Colorado*
Serve with:
PLATTER MACARONI
SLICED FRESH TOMATOES
INSTANT PUDDING (any flavor)

New Englanders settling in the Dakota territories brought this no-nonsense dish with them.

SIMPLE CHICKEN FRICASSEE

3 to 4 lb. chicken fryer pieces	1 small whole onion
salt and pepper	¼ c (½ stick) butter
1 t dried thyme	2 c water

Modern chickens contain so much fat, mainly hiding under the skin, that it's a good idea to skin chickens before cooking.

Dry chicken pieces, then rub with seasonings. Place in frying pan with rest of ingredients. Simmer 30 to 40 minutes until tender

If you want to make gravy, remove chicken to hot platter and cover with aluminum foil to keep warm. Remove onion from broth. Measure 1½ cups broth into a saucepan. Stir 3 to 4 tablespoons flour into ½ cup milk to make a smooth paste, then add to simmering broth. Stir and cook until thickened.

The Germans who helped settle North Dakota brought with them their skills in preparing sour cabbage and the sausages which had originated in their native Frankfurt.

WIENERS AND SAUERKRAUT

1 lb. wieners	1 (16 oz.) can sauerkraut

Spread the sauerkraut evenly in a skillet. Top with wieners, cover and cook slowly until heated through.

North Dakota is second only to Kansas in wheat production, and leads in durum wheat — the hard variety used for making spaghetti and macaroni.

PLATTER MACARONI

1 c dry macaroni	¼ c chili sauce
2 c American cheese, grated	½ c butter or margarine
2 to 4 T Worcestershire sauce	melted

While the macaroni is boiling, grate the cheese, measure the chili sauce and have the butter piping hot. Pour boiling water over a platter to heat, then spread out the cooked macaroni on the heated platter. Sprinkle over the cheese, sauces, salt and pepper. Drizzle butter over all, and mix with two forks until creamy. 6 servings.

OHIO — THE BUCKEYE STATE

Capital	Columbus
Elevation	433 ft. to 1550 ft
Population (1980)	10,791,000
(1990)	10,752,000
17th State	admitted March 1, 1803
Tree	Buckeye
Flower	Scarlet Carnation
Bird	Cardinal

WHILE IN OHIO...

CAMP in Ohio's State Parks with campgrounds — most of which are water-oriented and many deeply forested.

EXPLORE Mound City Group National Monument, or other mounds, odd-shaped earth structures built by ancestors of present-day Indians.

FISH in Lake Erie, or in numerous reservoirs and lakes for many varieties of fish including bass, pike, crappie and bluegill.

DRIFT along an Ohio river in a canoe, or climb aboard the sternwheeler, Delta Queen, for a Mississippi River cruise.

WANDER through Village Restorations, which include Schoenbrunn Village, founded in 1772; and Ohio Village, depicting a 19th century town.

TOUR the U.S. Air Force Museum and trace the history of aviation from the Wright brothers to modern space travel.

VISIT the Professional Football Hall of Fame in Canton.

FIND the homes, birthplaces or memorials of seven U.S. presidents.

★ ★ ★ ★ ★ ★

WRITE for more information: Ohio Division of Travel and Tourism, 77 S. High Street, 29th Floor, Columbus, OH 43215.

TRY

CINCINNATI PORK CHOPS
or
CAMPERS' DELIGHT
or
SUE'S SOUPER FAST CHICKEN POT PIE, see South Dakota
serve with
BROCCOLI, ZUCCHINI, CUCUMBER STICKS with
BUTTERMILK DRESSING FOR DUNKING
SPICY APPLESAUCE

Cincinnati, one of the earliest distribution centers for the fast-growing transportation systems of the early 1800's, was nicknamed "Porkopolis" because of the number of hogs shipped from there.

CINCINNATI PORK CHOPS

6 pork chops
1 small onion, sliced
3 or 4 carrots, diced
3 med. potatoes, diced
salt and pepper
1 t sage (optional)
2 c hot water
1 T gravy browner

Brown chops slightly on both sides in a large skillet. Remove, then lightly brown vegetables in same pan. Push vegetables to one side; place three pork chops in bottom of pan; cover with vegetables, then lay remaining chops on top. Add seasonings to hot water and pour over all, lifting bottom chops so water seeps under. Simmer gently for about 45 minutes, or until chops are done. Place meat on platter and spoon vegetables on each. Thicken gravy with 2 tablespoons flour mixed with ¼ cup cold water, add browner, then pour over meat and vegetables.

The originator of this recipe notes: "The delight of this dish while camping is only a skillet to wash."

CAMPER'S DELIGHT

1 lb. bulk pork sausage
½ med. head cabbage, thinly sliced
6 med. potatoes, sliced
2 med. onions, sliced

Brown sausage in skillet; drain off most fat. Add rest of ingredients and cook until vegetables are tender, about 30 minutes. 6 servings.

★ Evelyn Sliger, Sidney, OH

BUTTERMILK DRESSING

1 c buttermilk
1 c mayonnaise
½ t salt
2 t parsley flakes
1 t garlic powder
1/8 t pepper
½ t oregano
½ t basil

Stir all ingredients together. Keep in covered container in the refrigerator.

For a dip, add chopped green onion and thinly grated carrot for color.

SPICY APPLESAUCE

Dust canned applesauce with cinnamon, or stir in a handful of red hot candies for a spicy surprise.

OKLAHOMA — THE SOONER STATE

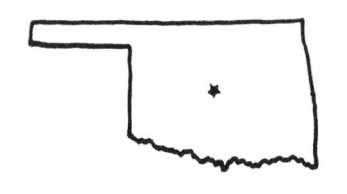

Capital	Oklahoma City
Elevation	287 ft. to 4973 ft.
Population (1980)	3,177,000
(1990)	3,305,000
46th State	admitted Nov. 16, 1907
Tree	Redbud
Flower	Mistletoe
Bird	Flycatcher

WHILE IN OKLAHOMA ...

CAMP in some State Parks where novel "Rent-a-Teepee" programs include cots, mattresses and battery lanterns.

VISIT the National Hall of Fame for Famous American Indians; National Cowboy Hall of Fame and Western Heritage Center; Tsa-La-Gi, a 17th-century re-created Cherokee Village; treasured Indian Museums.

TOUR Har-ber Village with 82 buildings and recreations of an early day frontier town; a double log cabin or an 1899 Queen Anne style home.

STEP farther back in time when viewing the Runestone, believed carved by Vikings; and still farther back at Black Mesa's dinosaur pits and tracks.

VIEW the nation's only capitol with an oil well under it and a derrick in front; then explore rugged mountains, pine forests, great plains.

RELIVE the silent movie era at the Tom Mix museum; or recapture the humor of Will Rogers at daily film showings at his Memorial.

FISH in the world's largest concentration of man-made lakes for largemouth and white bass, catfish, sunfish, crappie and more.

★ ★ ★ ★ ★ ★

WRITE for more information: Tourism and Recreation Dept., 500 Will Rogers Building, Oklahoma City, OK 73105.

TRY

SPANISH BEANS
or
CAMPFIRE STEAK
or
LUNCHEON MEAT BARBECUE, *see Iowa*
serve with
CHUCKWAGON BISCUITS
VEGETABLE MEDLEY, *see Oregon*
FRESH FRUIT or MELONS

Although the Indian influence is strong in Oklahoma, whose name translates to "Land of the Redskin", and whose official seal is a composite of the five Indian nations, Cherokee, Creek, Chocotaw, Chicasaw, and Seminole, there is often a Spanish touch to Oklahoman cookery.

SPANISH BEANS

½ lb. bacon, cut into strips (crosswise)
2 bell peppers, in thin strips
1 (16 oz.) can whole tomatoes
½ bay leaf
1 t chili powder
1 c grated cheddar cheese
1 (16 oz.) can kidney beans

Fry bacon in a saucepan until crisp. Remove and pour off all but 2 tablespoons fat. Add peppers to the fat and cook slowly until tender, but do not brown. Add tomatoes and mash or cut into pulp. Stir in bay leaf and chili powder. Add beans and simmer slowly for 30 minutes to blend flavors. Remove bay leaf. Serve on heated platter with bacon and cheese sprinkled on top.

Cowboys are such an important part of Oklahoma's history that a monument to them stands in front of the capitol building. One of the staples of these range-riders' diets was:

CAMPFIRE STEAK

Rib or sirloin steaks
garlic salt or salt and pepper

Hold a steak sideways, and rub the grill with the fat along the edge. Sprinkle garlic salt or salt and pepper on both sides of steaks, then place on a grill over a hot (preferably wood) fire. Depending on the thickness of the steak, broil each side:

4-6 minutes for rare
7-8 minutes for medium
8-10 minutes for well done

If you'd like to try the chuckwagon cook's method of fixing biscuits, try this:

CHUCKWAGON BISCUITS

Biscuit dough from your favorite biscuit mix
Oil

When the dough has been mixed and kneaded, flour your hands well, then pinch off enough dough to make 1½-inch balls. Flatten slightly and drop into hot oil in a heavy skillet. Use enough oil so pan is covered about 1/8-inch deep. Turn biscuits when raised and dark brown on one side. Cover pan and cook about five minutes more.

OREGON — THE BEAVER STATE

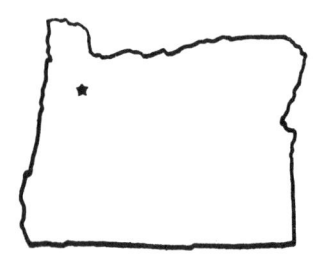

Capital	Salem
Elevation	sea level to 11,235 ft.
Population (1980)	2,549,000
(1990)	2,698,000
33rd State	admitted Feb. 14, 1859
Tree	Douglas Fir
Flower	Oregon Grape
Bird	Meadowlark

WHILE IN OREGON...

- **CAMP** — in any of over 50 State Parks — along the 400-mile coast; in mountains, on rivers; or in Crater Lake National Park.
- **TOUR** — elegant 19th century homes; find the replica of Lewis and Clark's original settlement; photograph the 235 foot monolith, Haystack Rock.
- **OBSERVE** — cheesemaking from viewing windows; watch commercial fishing activities and visit fish canneries; descend beneath the sea to a natural aquarium.
- **VIEW** — waterfalls and volcanic cones; hunt for agates, thundereggs and other semi-precious stones; visit a reindeer ranch; attend a Timber Carnival.
- **ENJOY** — Shakespeare in mountain-encircled Ashland; watch craftsmen turn rough native myrtlewood into satin-finish artifacts.
- **SKI** — all year long on Mt. Hood; in the winter choose from 13 resorts; go cross-country in vast mountainous areas.
- **FISH** — for salmon, steelhead and trout in more than 50,000 rivers and streams, in 1600 lakes, in coastal bays; look for shellfish along the coastline.

★ ★ ★ ★ ★ ★ ★

- **WRITE** — for more information: Oregon Tourism Division, 775 Summer St., NE, Salem, OR 97310.

TRY

KITCHEN STOVE CLAMBAKE
or
MARINATED SALMON STEAKS, *see Alaska*
or
BRAISED CHICKEN, *see Rhode Island*
serve with
SHEEPHERDER'S POTATOES, *see Nevada*
VEGETABLE MEDLEY
SUMMER PUDDING

Since all accessible beaches in Oregon are open to the public's "free and unobstructed use" — the Western Coast is a good place to try:

KITCHEN STOVE CLAMBAKE

Wet seaweed, well washed	1½ lb. lobster
2 c water	4 ears corn, husked
4 large potatoes	12 steamer clams
2½-3 lb. chicken pieces	

Fill the bottom of a large enamel pot with a layer of seaweed. Add water and place over high heat. Meanwhile, wrap potatoes and corn in aluminum foil. Wrap each chicken piece in cheesecloth.

When water boils, add potatoes and cover with seaweed, cover. 15 minutes later, add the chicken and another layer of seaweed, cover.

15 minutes later, add the lobster and more seaweed; cover. About 8 minutes later add the corn. 10 minutes later add the clams. Cover and steam until clams open. Serve with butter and kettle liquid as a dip. 4 servings.

★ Rita Starr Conlin, Hartford, CT

Vegetables seem more flavorful when cooked in combination, so develop your own medley with whatever you have on hand.

VEGETABLE MEDLEY

2 T butter or margarine or 2 slices bacon, fried until crisp	vegetables, fresh and/or canned

Stir fry in butter or bacon grease a combination of fresh celery, bell pepper, onions, broccoli, carrots, cauliflower, zucchini ... until crisp-tender. Add a can of mushrooms, canned green beans, corn. Stir in a diced tomato and simmer to blend flavors. Salt and pepper to taste.

The profusion of blackberries in Oregon was a welcome sight to early trail-weary pioneers, who turned them into:

SUMMER PUDDING

Stew blackberries gently with a bit of sugar until juicy. Arrange layers of buttered white bread (firm is best) and the berries in a deep bowl. Weight down with a plate set on top of the pudding to let the juice seep into the bread. Chill and serve with cream.

PENNSYLVANIA — THE KEYSTONE STATE

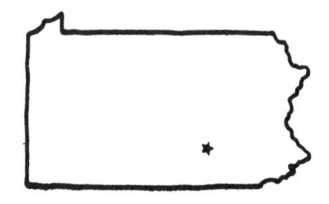

Capital	Harrisburg
Elevation	sea level to 3213 ft.
Population (1980)	11,865,000
(1990)	11,888,000
2nd State	admitted Dec. 12, 1787
Tree	Hemlock
Flower	Mountain Laurel
Bird	Ruffed Grouse

WHILE IN PENNSYLVANIA...

CAMP in State Parks, including Hearts Content State Park with trout streams, forest land, and spectacular views; or in Ricketts Glen, with 33 waterfalls.

GLOW with patriotic pride at Independence Hall, Liberty Bell Shrine, Valley Forge, Washington Crossing, Betsy Ross House, Gettysburg.

VISIT unique museums — Antique Music, Mummers, Canal, Mushroom, Wedgewood; or walk through a two-story model of a human heart at Franklin Institute.

VIEW the unbelievable: wild ducks walking on top of fish at Pymatuning Lake; or 20-foot long, 3-foot wide icicles which grow in summer and melt in winter.

MAKE the most of any of 227 Covered "Kissing" Bridges; or take a romantic cruise on an old-fashioned riverboat on the Beautiful Ohio.

FIND the heritage from the Five Nations of Indians in their magical-sounding names: Allegheny, Monongahela, Punxsatawney, Susquehanna, Wyalusing, Youghiogeny.

WANDER through Lancaster's Farmers' Market, continuous since 1870; explore the world of the Pennsylvania Dutch, in Amish and Mennonite communities.

FISH for black bass, muskellunge, four varieties of trout, northern pike and more, or catch the shad run on the Delaware River in spring.

WRITE for more information: State Board of Tourism, 453 Forum Building, Harrisburg, PA 17120.

TRY

CHICKEN CORN SOUP
or
PORK POT PIE
or
CAMPERS' DELIGHT, see *Ohio*
serve with
HOT GARLIC BREAD
CARROT AND RAISIN SALAD
SHOOFLY PIE
(if you feel like baking — *FRESH FRUIT*, if not)

While Pennsylvania Pepper-Pot is the most famous of Pennsylvania soups, it takes hours to prepare; so we've settled for second best, with some short-cuts for travelers.

CHICKEN CORN SOUP

6 c chicken broth
4 stalks celery, sliced
2 med. onions, diced
1 (16 oz.) cream-style corn
1 (12½ oz.) can chunked chicken
1 c uncooked wide noodles
salt and pepper

Simmer celery and onions in broth, seasoned with pepper, for about 20 minutes. Add corn and noodles, bring to a boil, then simmer until noodles are nearly done, about 8 minutes. Stir in chicken and cook for another 5 minutes. 4 servings

Mennonites, a religious sect of German origin, were recruited by William Penn to help establish his colony. Their pot pies were unusual because the "pies" had no top crusts — homemade noodles were simmered in the broth.

PORK POT PIE

2 lbs. boneless pork
2 T oil
5 c chicken broth
2 med. potatoes, thinly sliced
1 large carrot, sliced
1 c chopped celery
salt and pepper
4 or 5 lasagna noodles, uncooked

Cut pork into 1-inch cubes, removing visible fat. Cook in oil in a large saucepan until no longer pink. Add rest of ingredients, except noodles, and simmer, covered, for 10 minutes. Bring to a brisk boil and add lasagna noodles, broken into squares. Cook 10 to 12 minutes until noodles are tender. 4-6 servings.

It's easy to assume that this pie was named because the bubbled-out drops of molasses attracted flies which had to be "shooed".

SHOOFLY PIE

Crumb Mixture:
1½ c flour
½ c brown sugar, packed
½ t cinnamon
¼ c butter or margarine

Filling:
¾ c hot water
¾ c light molasses
½ t baking soda
1 9-inch unbaked pie shell

For the crumb mixture, combine flour, sugar and cinnamon. Cut in butter until the mixture resembles coarse bread crumbs.

Dissolve molasses in hot water and add soda. Spoon one third into pie shell, cover with one third crumb mixture. Repeat two more times.

Bake for 10 minutes in a 450° oven, turn heat down to 350° and bake 30 minutes longer.

RHODE ISLAND — THE OCEAN STATE

Capital	Providence
Elevation	sea level to 812 ft.
Population (1980)	958,000
(1990)	973,000
13th State	admitted May 29, 1790
Tree	Red Maple
Flower	Violet
Bird	Rhode Island Red

WHILE IN RHODE ISLAND...

CAMP in State Parks — in wooded areas near a pond; on the Appalachian Trail, just ½ mile from an Atlantic beach; or in a remote canoe park.

DISCOVER national "firsts" — schoolhouse, Quaker meetinghouse, synagogue, First Baptist Meetinghouse, cotton mill, and Norse Tower, believed built by Vikings in 1000 AD.

WATCH a blacksmith at work, smell herb gardens, admire antique barns and farming equipment in working farms, some dating from the 1700's.

TAKE the children to a "hands-on" museum of their own, or let them attend special events, from Sand Castle Contests to a Kid's Dog Show.

WANDER through The Arcade, the nation's oldest indoor shopping center and a fine example of Greek Revival Architecture.

ADMIRE clapboard cottages around village greens, or opulent European-style mansions and gardens, including Green Animals Topiary Gardens.

FISH without a license in tranquil bay waters, the sounds, or in the Atlantic. Saltwater fish include tuna, striped bass, cod, tautog.

★ ★ ★ ★ ★ ★

WRITE for more information: Rhode Island Tourism & Promotion Division, 7 Jackson Walkway, Providence, RI 02903.

TRY

BRAISED CHICKEN
or
KEDGEREE
or
CLAM CHOWDER, see *Massachusetts*
serve with
HOT GREEN BEAN SALAD
SUCCOTASH, see *New Jersey*
BLUEBERRY PIE, see *Connecticut*

With the Rhode Island Red as the state bird, it's no wonder that chicken is available in so many places — supermarkets, country stores, sometimes farms advertise their sale. Watch for a sign.

BRAISED CHICKEN

1 (2½-3½ lb.) fryer 1 t salt
½ c flour 3 T oil or shortening
1 t paprika (optional) water

Dredge chicken pieces in flour seasoned with salt and paprika. Brown chicken slowly in shortening or oil in a heavy frying pan. (Browning is important to produce optimum flavor.) When browned, add about one cup water. Cover and cook over low heat about 45 minutes, until chicken is tender. 6 servings.

Adapted from an East Indian dish, this Rhode Island version leaves out the hot curry condiments of the original — but you might experiment with spices to your liking.

RHODE ISLAND KEDGEREE

2 c cooked rice 2 T butter or margarine
4 hard-cooked eggs, chopped salt and pepper
1 c cooked, flaked white fish

If you start with freshly cooked rice (1 cup rice in 2 cups boiling water), just stir in the fish, eggs, butter and seasonings and heat gently. However, if it's cold rice you have put a little water in the saucepan, add the rice and steam on low heat; then proceed as above.

CLAM CHOWDER, see MASSACHUSETTS

The use of Narraganset clams and leaving the chowder liquid thin, instead of thickening with crackers, changes the Cape Cod version into a more typical "Little Rhody" dish.

HOT GREEN BEAN SALAD

3 slices bacon, 1 (16 oz.) can green beans
 cut in 1" pieces dash of pepper
2 T flour 2 green onions, cut into
3 T vinegar   ½ inch lengths

Saute bacon until crisp. Drain away all but 2 tablespoons bacon fat. Stir in flour and stir until brown. Add vinegar and undrained beans, stirring until sauce thickens. Stir in onion just before serving. 6 servings.

SOUTH CAROLINA — THE PALMETTO STATE

Capital	Columbia
Elevation	sea level to 3,560 ft.
Population (1980)	3,203,000
(1990)	3,377,000
8th state	admitted May 23, 1788
Tree	Palmetto
Flower	Carolina Jessamine
Bird	Carolina Wren

WHILE IN SOUTH CAROLINA...

CAMP   in State Parks, with sites by the ocean, on rivers, under moss-draped oaks, near a frontier homestead

FISH   in lakes, rivers, streams for a variety of fish, from catfish to whiting, or from a pier or jetty onto the Atlantic (no saltwater license required).

WANDER   through Gardens. The state's most famous are Middleton Place and Magnolia. There are also Swan Lake Iris, Cypress, Brookgreen and Glencairn Gardens -- the latter featuring azaleas and dogwoods. Clemson University Botanical Garden displays over 2000 varieties of plants.

WALK   on an elevated boardwalk to see alligators swim in a swampy depression called a "Carolina Bay" — believed formed by a meteor.

RIDE   through Charleston in a horse-drawn carriage to admire hundreds of pre-revolutionary, late 18th century and pre-1840 beautiful Victorian buildings.

TOUR   Fort Sumter where the first shot of the Civil War was fired. It rises from the depths of Charleston Harbor and boat tours are available.

VISIT   Columbia, South Carolina's capital. One of the first planned communities in the nation, the city was established in 1786.

★ ★ ★ ★ ★ ★

WRITE   for more information: Division of Tourism, P.O. Box 71, Columbia, S.C. 29202-0071.

TRY

GRAND STRAND CHICKEN BOG
or
CATFISH STEW
or
SHRIMP GUMBO, see *Mississippi*
serve with
HOPPING JOHN
GREEN BEAN AND ONION SALAD, see *Delaware*
FRESH FRUIT

The 55 miles of beaches stretching along South Carolina's coast is known as the Grand Strand. Cooks from throughout the area gather each spring to compete in a "chicken bog" contest.

GRAND STRAND CHICKEN BOG

2½ lb. chicken pieces   1½ lb. smoked sausage
1 c chopped onion   1 t black pepper
4 c water   2 c long grain rice

Boil chicken and onions in water until tender. If desired, debone chicken. Slice sausage in ½" pieces. Add sausage and rice to chicken. Simmer until all broth is absorbed and rice is cooked. (About 25 minutes). Serves 8.

A favorite of South Carolinians since plantation days is:

CATFISH STEW

6 med. freshwater fish or catfish, cut into small pieces
2 (10 oz.) cans condensed tomato soup
1 sm. bottle tomato catsup   ½ stick butter
¼ lb. salt pork, diced   1 T pepper
1 lrg. onion, sliced thin   Dash cayenne
Few drops Worcestershire sauce 1 T salt

Combine soup and catsup and boil slowly. Fry salt pork and saute onions until tender. Add with all other ingredients, except fish, plus 1 cup water if too thick. Boil 5 minutes. Drop in fish and cook about 5 more minutes.

This dish originated in South Carolina, and is now a traditional New Year's dish throughout the South. 'Tis said, "Eat peas on New Year's Day to have plenty of everything the rest of the year."

HOPPING JOHN

4 slices bacon, diced   1 t salt
½ c uncooked rice   1 (16 oz.) can Black-Eyed
1 c water   Peas

In a large frying pan, brown bacon then pour off most of the fat. Stir in rice; add water and salt. Cover and cook 14 minutes. Add black-eyed peas and heat. 4 servings.

BANANA SANDWICH

Cut ripe bananas into ¼ inch slices. Insert between ginger snaps or vanilla wafers. Press gently.

SOUTH DAKOTA — THE COYOTE STATE

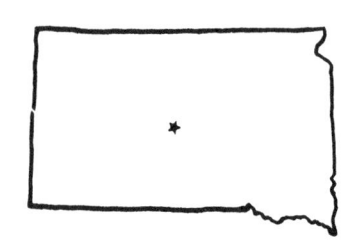

Capital	Pierre
Elevation	962 ft. t0 7242 ft.
Population (1980)	691,000
(1990)	708,000
40th State	admitted Nov. 2, 1889
Tree	Black Hills Spruce
Flower	Pasqueflower
Bird	Pheasant

WHILE IN SOUTH DAKOTA...

CAMP in National Parks or State Parks, including fabulous Custer State Park in the Black Hills — second largest in the nation.

DRIVE leisurely on Iron Mountain Road from Custer to Mt. Rushmore through the "tunnel-windows" which frame the Shrine of Democracy.

EXPLORE the 4th and 8th-longest caves in the world: Jewel and Wind Caves with their incredible formations of "popcorn", "frostwork" and "balloons".

SHARE the pride and dignity of the Sioux at a PowWow, at the still unfinished mountain sculpture of Crazy Horse, at many Indian Museums.

CLIMB on prehistoric mammoth reptiles in Dinosaur Park; visit Calamity Jane's and Wild Bill Hickok's Deadwood; join in the excitement of a Rodeo.

VIEW the world's only Corn Palace with minarets of grain and corn mosaics that change every year — a harvest tradition from early statehood.

FISH in the "Great Lakes" of South Dakota — four huge reservoirs along the Missouri River; in glacial lakes or mountain streams.

★ ★ ★ ★ ★ ★

WRITE for more information: South Dakota Tourism, 711 Wells Ave., Pierre, SD 57501-3369.

TRY

GRILLED BRATWURST
or
SUE'S "SOUPER" FAST CHICKEN POT PIE
or
PORK CHOPS WITH STUFFING, see *Idaho*
serve with
HOT POTATO SALAD
CUCUMBER and CELERY STICKS
KUCHEN from a bakery

Hardworking farm women who helped settle South Dakota under the Homestead Act in the 1800's developed one-pot meals that required little watching. Our contributor continues the time-saving tradition by using convenience foods in:

SUE'S "SOUPER" FAST CHICKEN POT PIE
2 (10½ oz.) cans cream of chicken soup
1 small can evaporated milk
2 (8 oz.) cans chopped chicken or 2 c leftover chicken
1 (12 oz.) pkg. frozen or 1 can (16 oz.) mixed vegetables
salt and pepper, to taste
1 can refrigerator biscuits, unbaked

Combine all ingredients except biscuits in a casserole. Bake at 350° until hot and bubbly. Remove from oven and top with biscuits. Increase heat to 400°, return to oven and bake until biscuits are brown, about 15 minutes.

★ Linda Sue Croney Aten, Virginia Beach, VA

Make: SKILLET CHICKEN WITH DUMPLINGS. Heat all ingredients except biscuits in a skillet. Bring to a boil; place biscuits on top; turn heat to medium; cover and cook about 15 minutes until biscuits turn into light, feathery dumplings.

Midwest cookery owes much to the influx of German immigrants during the last half of the 19th century. The Germans' expertise in sausage-making soon introduced a wide variety of succulent "wursts" one of the best being a BRAT.

GRILLED BRATWURST
6 bratwurst

Either grill bratwursts over coals, or brown slowly in a heavy skillet until thoroughly cooked. Being careful not to cut completely through, split each bratwurst lengthwise. Flatten out on individual plates, and heap with HOT POTATO SALAD.

Another German contribution is serving potato salad hot.

HOT POTATO SALAD
½ lb. bacon   1 t sugar
⅓ c vinegar, diluted   1 t salt, ¼ t pepper
  with water to make ½ cup   5 c cooked potatoes, diced
1 fork-whipped egg   ½ c onion, chopped

In a large skillet, fry bacon until crisp; remove and crumble. Pour off bacon fat, reserving ⅓ cup. Put the measured drippings back into the skillet, and stir in vinegar, egg and seasonings. Heat slowly, stirring constantly until thickened. Add potatoes, onion and bacon. Toss gently while heating through. 6 servings.

TENNESSEE — THE VOLUNTEER STATE

Capital	Nashville
Elevation	182 ft. to 6,643 ft.
Population (1980)	4,651,000
(1990)	4,803,000
16th state	admitted June 1, 1796
Tree	Poplar
Flower	Iris
Bird	Mockingbird

WHILE IN TENNESSEE...

CAMP — in State Parks, many feature historic sites, Indian Mounds, Davy Crockett's birthplace, restored forts from the Revolutionary and Civil Wars.

EXPLORE — the Great Smoky Mountains which contain part of the Appalachian Trail, and more than 1300 varieties of trees, shrubs and flowering plants.

FISH — in man-made lakes, trout streams, and many rivers including the mighty Mississippi.

SKI — even in summer on the world's largest artificial ski surface.

ASCEND — to the top of Lookout Mountain and view seven states; descend 1,120 feet inside to marvel at the 145 ft. underground waterfall.

WATCH — a recording session at the Country Music Hall of Fame complex, or attend a mountain Crafts Fair to see dulcimer makers, potters, woodcarvers.

TOUR — the "Hermitage", Andrew Jackson's home; or the Tennessee State Capitol, completed in 1854; or an exact reproduction of Athen's famous Parthenon, or the Great American Pyramid in Memphis.

VISIT — a variety of museums — from a knife museum to a Steamboat experience; from Railroad Museums to the American Museum of Science and Energy.

★ ★ ★ ★ ★ ★

WRITE — for more information: Tennessee Tourist Development, P.O. Box 23170, Room TM, Nashville, TN 37202.

TRY

PAN FRIED CAT FISH
with HUSH PUPPIES
or
FRIED HAM AND RED-EYE GRAVY, see *Virginia*
or
GRILLED LEMON CHICKEN, see *Colorado*
serve with:
BOILED RICE
PINEAPPLE COLESLAW, see *Virginia*
SOUTH FULTON BANANA PUDDING

If you can't get to Tennessee in April for the "World's Largest Fish Fry" (which uses 1,325 pounds of corn meal, 212 pounds of salt and 8,500 pounds of catfish!), you'll just have to fry your own.

PAN FRIED CATFISH

Catfish fillets   Oil
White cornmeal   Salt

Pat the catfish dry. Dip in cornmeal and salt mixed together. Place in hot skillet wth oil about 1/8" deep. Fry briefly over medium heat, turning carefully when golden brown on one side, then brown other side. This takes about 10 minutes total.

Traditionally served with fried fish, these corn cakes were possibly stirred up to feed the whining dogs by some weary cook who then found them "mighty good eating" for humans.

HUSH PUPPIES

2 c white cornmeal   1 egg, beaten
2 t baking powder   ¼ c water
1½ t salt   ¾ c milk
¼ t pepper   2 T minced onion

Combine dry ingredients in a large bowl. Mix together the egg, water and milk. Add to dry ingredients and stir until smooth. Add the onions. After the fish is fried, remove from skillet and add cooking oil to the fat in the pan so it is about ¼ inch deep. To the hot oil, drop teaspoonfuls of hush-puppy mixture. Fry until golden brown, turning once. Drain on paper towels. Makes about 3 dozen.

Before modern methods of refrigeration, South Fulton, Tennessee and its twin city Fulton, Kentucky, were redistribution centers for 70% of all bananas brought into the United States. Highlight of the four-day festival honoring this proud history, is a 2,000 pound banana pudding serving 10,000 people.

You can celebrate this unusual event with the same recipe, scaled down to family size.

SOUTH FULTON BANANA PUDDING

3 sliced bananas   Vanilla wafers
1 pkg. Vanilla Instant Pudding, prepared according to package directions.

Layer an 8x8-inch square pan with vanilla wafers. Cover with a single layer of sliced bananas, then with vanilla pudding. Continue alternating layers — ending with wafers. Chill, enjoy. 4 to 6 servings.

TEXAS — THE LONE STAR STATE

Capital	Austin
Elevation	sea level to 8751 ft.
Population (1980)	15,280,000
(1990)	16,685,000
28th State	admitted Dec. 29, 1845
Tree	Pecan
Flower	Bluebonnet
Bird	Mockingbird

WHILE IN TEXAS ...

CAMP   in some of the 110 State Parks or at Rio Grande Campground in Big Bend National Park.

VISIT   major Theme Parks such as Astro World, Sea World or Six Flags. Or view underwater mysteries at the State Aquarium or cosmic wonders at NASA.

CATCH   Pinto Bean and Chili Cookoffs, Texas Rice Festival, Peanut Fest, Shrimporee, Citrus Fiesta, Jackpot Roping, Starving Artists' Show.

TAKE   a driving tour of the capital and include People's Renaissance Market, Treaty Oak, and the O. Henry Museum.

GAZE   in awe at 90 peaks towering more than a mile high when you motor through the "Alps of Texas".

FEEL   the heart of Texas in its Shrine of Independence — the Alamo, and follow the Mission Trail which predates California's.

FISH   over 6,000 square miles of inland freshwater plus scores of tidal bays and 624 miles of shoreline along the Gulf Coast.

★ ★ ★ ★ ★ ★

WRITE   for more information: Texas Department of Commerce -- Tourism Division, Box 12728, Capitol Station, Austin, TX 78711.

TRY

DOROTHY'S TEXAS CHILI
or
PAPRIKA CHICKEN WITH NOODLES
or
SAUTEED POMPANO
ALMOST BAKED POTATOES, *see Washington*
serve with
TOSSED GREEN SALAD
HOT GARLIC BREAD
TEXAS AMBROSIA

While most Texas Chili is hot, hot; and some purists insist on chopped (not ground) beef; the variations are endless.

DOROTHY'S TEXAS CHILI

1½ lbs. ground beef	1 (16 oz.) can tomatoes
1 (16 oz.) can tomato juice	½ med. onion, chopped
1 (16 oz.) can kidney beans	1-3 T chili powder
½ bell pepper, chopped	salt and pepper

Cook ground beef until brown and crumbly. Add remaining ingredients and simmer 1½ to 2 hours.

★ Dorothy Burgess, Huntsville, TX

Refugees from the Hungarian Revolution of 1848 introduced paprika to American cuisine.

PAPRIKA CHICKEN

1 (3-3½ lb.) fryer chicken	1 T paprika
1 T butter or margarine	½ t salt
½ c onion, chopped	dash of pepper
¼ c water	½ c dairy sour cream
1 (8 oz.) can tomato sauce	2 T flour

In a large skillet, slowly brown chicken pieces in butter. Remove chicken, add onions and cook until tender. Stir in 2 tablespoons water, tomato sauce and seasonings. Place chicken back in skillet, cover and simmer until done — about 35 to 40 minutes. Blend sour cream with flour and remaining 2 T of water. Pour over chicken mixture; cook and stir until thick. Do not boil. 4 servings.

Pompano is called the King of Fish and is plentiful in the Gulf of Mexico waters, so try:

SAUTEED POMPANO

4 small pompano	flour for coating fish
½ c milk	2 T oil
salt	2 T butter or margarine

Dip fish into milk which has been poured into a flat bowl. Roll fish in flour. Saute in hot oil and butter until fish is golden on each side and flakes easily (4-5 minutes per side). Pass wedges of lemon.

Once THE Christmas dessert of Texas, this is prettiest served from a glass bowl.

TEXAS AMBROSIA

Allow about ½ large orange and about ¼ cup coconut per person. Peel and cut oranges crosswise into thin slices. Layer orange slices in the bottom of a bowl, sprinkle lightly with sugar, then cover with shredded coconut. Repeat layers, ending with coconut. Best when chilled several hours.

UTAH — THE BEEHIVE STATE

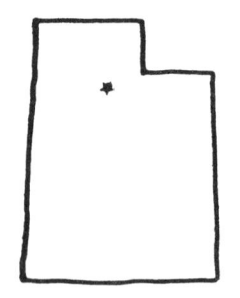

Capital	Salt Lake City
Elevation	2000 ft. to 13,528 ft.
Population (1980)	1,554,000
(1990)	1,665,000
45th State	admitted Jan 4, 1896
Tree	Blue Spruce
Flower	Sego Lily
Bird	Seagull

WHILE IN UTAH...

CAMP in National Parks: Arches, Zion, Bryce Canyon, Capitol Reef, Canyonlands; or choose among 44 State Parks.

FIND Auto Speed Record signs along the Bonneville Salt Flats, then float like a cork in the Great Salt Lake.

SEE the Golden Spike site at Promontory, with working replicas of the two engines which came together here and joined East and West by rail.

SPEND time in Salt Lake City at Temple Square, hearing the famed Tabernacle Choir and massive organ; then to Trolley Square.

FEAST your eyes on canyon and mesa vistas, frolicking stones in Goblin Valley, natural bridges, towering spires of eroded sculpture.

HIKE to Nine-mile Canyon to study ancient Indians' Petroglyphs and Pictographs, or visit Dinosaur Gardens with 14 life-size replicas.

FISH and enjoy other water sports in the movie-famous "Color Country" of the Colorado River, Lake Powell, and several side canyons.

★ ★ ★ ★ ★ ★

WRITE for more information: Utah Travel Council, Council Hall/Capitol Hill, Salt Lake City, UT 84114.

TRY

MORMON SPLIT PEA SOUP
or
CHILI-MAC
or
PORK CHOPS WITH STUFFING, see *Idaho*
serve with
CHUCKWAGON BISCUITS, See *Oklahoma*
CARROT AND RAISIN SALAD
COVERED WAGON CANDY

On their westward trek, Mormons prepared an unusual split pea soup — using ground pork shaped into balls instead of the traditional ham. You can shorten preparation time by using canned soup and pork link sausages.

MORMON SPLIT PEA SOUP

2 (10½ oz.) cans split pea soup
1 (8 oz.) pkg. pork sausage links
2 medium raw potatoes, peeled and diced

Cut sausages into 1-inch chunks. Brown in a large saucepan; pour off fat and add pea soup, diluted according to can directions. Add potatoes and simmer until tender, about 20 minutes. 4-6 servings.

Some 50 or 60 years ago before hamburgers had been invented and nearly every drugstore in the country had a lunch counter, a favorite "drugstore lunch" was:

CHILI-MAC

1 c dry macaroni, cooked according to package directions
1 (16 oz.) can chili beans
1 small onion, chopped   shredded cheddar cheese

Cook macaroni and heat chili beans. Put a serving of hot macaroni on each plate, cover with chili and sprinkle with onions and cheese. 4-6 servings.

CARROT AND RAISIN SALAD

Peel and grate carrots into a bowl, stir in a handful of raisins, add mayonnaise and a splash of lemon juice to taste.

Dried fruit, prepared by the pioneers as candy, is similar to the trail mix carried by hikers today.

COVERED WAGON CANDY

2 c raisins   ¼ c walnuts,
⅔ c dates, pitted   coarsely chopped
½ c dried prunes, pitted   2 T orange juice
peel of ½ small orange   granulated sugar

It's easiest to run the fruit through a food grinder or processor, but if one is not available — just finely chop the fruit and orange peel, then blend with nuts and orange juice. Using a level tablespoon for each, roll into balls and then in sugar. These keep well in a covered container. Makes about 30.

VERMONT — THE GREEN MOUNTAIN STATE

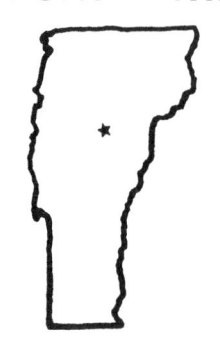

Capital	Montpelier
Elevation	95 ft. to 4,393 ft.
Population (1980)	516,000
(1990)	541,000
14th state	admitted March 4, 1791
Tree	Sugar Maple
Flower	Red Clover
Bird	Hermit Thrush

WHILE IN VERMONT...

CAMP in 38 State Park Campgrounds or choose the Green Mountain National Forest with its 260 mile footpath, "The Long Trail".

VISIT one of the granite quarries, then tour the State House at Montpelier, made of native granite and topped with a golden dome.

RELIVE history at Museums, including Shelburne with 45 acres of venerable structures, or Hidene, home of Abraham Lincoln's decendants until 1975.

FISH in Lake Champlain for salmon or trout, or try a trout stream. Watch the salmon run in a waterway bypass from observation windows.

COLLECT an antique at an auction, flea market or shop. Or tour the Craft Studios of weavers, potters, wood carvers and quilters.

EXPLORE Stowe's 6 mile recreation path or Moss Glen Falls.

SKI in any of over 31 ski areas including Stowe with 378 acres of skiable terrain.

★ ★ ★ ★ ★ ★

WRITE for more information: Vermont Chamber of Commerce, Dept. of Travel and Tourism, P.O. Box 37, Montpelier, VT 05602.

TRY

COLONIAL HASHED BEEF ON BUNS
or
SKILLET SCALLOPED POTATOES
with cold sliced ham
or
CHICKEN 'N NOODLES, see *Kansas*
serve with:
APPLE AND CELERY SALAD
MAPLE SYRUP TREAT

Wives of the Green Mountain Boys of Colonial days may have served this quickly prepared concoction. Notice the ingenious way the onion sauce is thickened and browned!

COLONIAL HASHED BEEF ON BUNS

1 large onion	1 lb. (½ inch thick) round steak
¼ c water (about)	2 T butter or margarine
¼ c beer (about)	Flour
salt and pepper	Buns

Cut onion in half, then cut into 1/8" slices. Simmer the onion in a small saucepan with water and beer to cover. Salt and pepper lightly. Meanwhile slice the steak into pieces about the size and width of your little finger. Roll the butter or margarine in flour (just dunk it in the cannister), and stir in a hot frying pan until the butter is melted and the flour browned. Add the steak, then the onion mixture, and simmer a few minutes until the sauce thickens. Serve over buns.

At one time people said that cows outnumbered people in Vermont. Try some Vermont cheese in this easy potato dish. Good with thinly sliced ham, or other cold cuts.

SKILLET SCALLOPED POTATOES

2½ c water	Salt and pepper to taste
2 T (or cubes) chicken bouillon	3 or 4 med. potatoes sliced into thin rounds
1 sm. onion, minced (or 1 T dried onion)	1 c fresh grated cheese

Heat water in skillet, dissolve bouillon, add onion, parsley and seasonings. Layer potatoes over onions, cover and simmer until potatoes are tender (about 20 minutes). Sprinkle with grated cheese. Replace lid and heat for a few minutes to melt cheese. Serves 4.

MAPLE SYRUP TREAT

If you're in Vermont in April at "sugarin'-off" time, try to attend a public sugar party. If a fresh snow fall occurs at the same time that the maple sap is being boiled into syrup, the syrup is drizzled onto mounds of snow, and sets into pools of delicious sweetness.

Wrong time of year? Make some dollar-size blueberry pancakes and drench them in maple syrup for a Vermont treat.

VIRGINIA — THE OLD DOMINION STATE

Capital	Richmond
Elevation	sea level to 5,729 ft.
Population (1980)	5,491,000
(1990)	5,787,000
10th state	admitted June 25, 1788
Tree	Dogwood
Flower	Dogwood
Bird	Cardinal

WHILE IN VIRGINIA...

CAMP at oceanfront Virginia Beach, with 28 miles of golden sand, or on the Eastern Shore, haven for snow geese and home of wild pony herds.

TRAVEL along the Blue Ridge Skyline Drive and Parkway and view Shenandoah Valley, tour Luray Caverns, or marvel at 215-foot high Natural Bridge.

CATCH a world-record fish in the Salt Water Fishing Tournament, or try for freshwater species in nearly 40 lakes, rivers, and streams.

TOUR Mt. Vernon, George Washington's plantation; and homes of Virginia's seven other presidents, incuding Monticello, Thomas Jefferson's architectural masterpiece.

RELIVE America's beginnings at Jamestown, at Yorktown, and at Colonial Williamsburg, largest restored 18th century town in America.

WATCH a Jousting Tournament; wander through The Old Country, ride a screaming roller coaster at Kings Dominion; or thrill to the Flying Circus' biplane stunts.

★ ★ ★ ★ ★ ★

WRITE for more information: Virginia Division of Tourism, 1021 East Cary Street, Richmond, VA 23219.

TRY

BRUNSWICK STEW
or
FRIED HAM WITH RED-EYE GRAVY
and *HOT BISCUITS*
or
CRAB PATTIES, *see Georgia*
serve with
BOILED RICE
PINEAPPLE COLE SLAW
COOKIES (your choice)

Originating in Brunswick County, Virginia, this stew was first made with nothing but squirrels and onions. As the settlers tamed the wilderness, more ingredients were added, and domesticated rabbit or chicken was substituted for squirrel. Traditionally served with cornbread, it is also good with thick slices of French bread.

BRUNSWICK STEW

3 to 4 lbs. chicken pieces
3 T butter or margarine
1 lrg. onion, minced
1 green pepper, minced
2½ c canned tomatoes
½ t ground thyme,
1 (8 oz.) can whole kernel corn
1 (8 oz.) can lima beans

Brown the chicken pieces in butter in a large skillet. Remove chicken and saute onion and pepper in the same pan just until soft. Return chicken to pan, add tomatoes and thyme. Simmer until chicken is almost tender (20 to 30 minutes). Add vegetables and simmer until heated through and chicken is done. 6 servings.

Serve this traditional southern dish with plenty of hot biscuits for mopping up the gravy, and send a silent thank you to the inventor of baking powder. Before this leavening agent was introduced, southerners beat their biscuit dough for at least half an hour to incorporate air for lightness!

FRIED HAM WITH RED-EYE GRAVY

4 slices ham (about ¼ inch thick)
2 or 3 T oil
1 c black coffee

Heat oil in heavy frying pan. Cook ham slices slowly until brown on each side. Remove from pan. To the hot pan add the coffee, stir and scrape pan bottom for one minute. Pour over ham.

PINEAPPLE COLE SLAW

To finely chopped cabbage, add 1 small can pineapple chunks, drained. Stir in mayonnaise, then trickle in some of the reserved pineapple juice until as moist as you like.

WASHINGTON — THE EVERGREEN STATE

Capital	Olympia
Elevation	sea level to 14,410 ft.
Population (1980)	4,245,000
(1990)	4,462,000
42nd State	admitted Nov. 11, 1889
Tree	Western Hemlock
Flower	Rhododendron
Bird	Western Goldfinch

WHILE IN WASHINGTON...

CAMP — in any of numerous State Parks, or choose from Washington's National Parks — Mount Rainier, Olympic or North Cascades.

TAKE — a ferry to the Olympic Peninsula for remote wilderness beauty; visit rain forests; the Norwegian town of Poulsbo; the enchanting San Juan Islands.

DIG — for clams in the intertidal zones of Juan de Fuca, Hood Canal, Puget Sound — also rich in oysters, crab and shrimp.

ATTEND — unique festivals: Sinterklass, Washington's Birthday Pow Wow, Bavarian Autumn Leaf, Lutefisk, and Meatball Dinner.

DISCOVER — why it's called the "Apple State" with a trip to Wenatchee and the Yakima Valley. Be sure to include Grand Coulee Dam.

CLIMB — or just admire the Cascades, including Mt. Rainier, Mt. St. Helens, and sister volcanoes, born of volcanic fire and glacial ice.

FISH — deep-sea or stream; water ski, swim, dive, sail off uncrowded beaches or in the Columbia and its several tributaries.

★ ★ ★ ★ ★ ★ ★

WRITE — for more information: State Board of Tourism, 101 General Administration Building, Olympia, WA 98504.

TRY

CHICKEN GABRIELLA
or
MARINATED SALMON, *see Alaska*
or
CAPE COD CLAM CHOWDER, *see Massachusetts*
serve with
ALMOST BAKED POTATOES
ZUCCHINI FRITATTA
APPLES AND CHEESE

Watching for breaks in the lava dams formed by the eruption of Mt. St. Helens was the lonely task of our contributor and her husband. Isolated in their trailer for many months of the year, the couple relied on canned goods and ingenuity for tasty dishes.

CHICKEN GABRIELLA

1 med. onion, thinly sliced
1 (10½ oz.) chunked chicken
1 (8 oz.) can tomato sauce
1 sauce can water
½ envelope dry onion soup mix
2 T brown sugar
2 T soy sauce
salt and pepper

Arrange onion on the bottom of a greased casserole. Layer chicken over the onion. Combine rest of ingredients and pour over chicken. Cover with foil. Bake in 350° oven about 20 to 30 minutes, until bubbly.

★ Merless George, Silverlake, WA

If you don't want to heat the oven, but like the mealiness of baked potatoes, you can achieve almost the same effect with:

ALMOST BAKED POTATOES

Scrub potatoes well; put in a heavy saucepan; cover with cold water and boil until done. Pour off water, put in two tablespoons butter or margarine. Turn heat to low, and let potatoes "bake" for about 5 minutes, shaking the pan occasionally — a little browning might occur, but that just improves the taste.

Any state that has a zucchini festival (which Washington does) deserves this excellent fritatta. The camper who shares this recipe says she likes to make it the evening before a trip, wrap it in aluminum foil, and refrigerate. With its high egg content, the family enjoys it for their first breakfast on the road. (Reheated or cold)

ZUCCHINI FRITATTA

4 T oil
1 onion, diced
2 medium zucchini
6 eggs
¼ t salt
¼ t pepper
½ t sweet basil
1 t dried parsley
¼ c grated parmesan
2 T butter or margarine

In a 10 inch round frying pan, saute onion over medium heat until limp. Add thinly sliced zucchini and brown with onion. In a large mixing bowl, beat eggs slightly, add rest of ingredients (except butter), blend well. Stir in zucchini and onion.

Melt butter in same frying pan, pour in zucchini-egg mixture. Cook uncovered, for 15 to 20 minutes. Cut in wedges to serve, or turn out of pan whole (See comment above.)

★ Linda Parsons, Pioneer, CA

WEST VIRGINIA — THE MOUNTAIN STATE

Capital	Charleston
Elevation	240 ft. to 4,862 ft.
Population (1980)	1,948,000
(1990)	1,918,000
35th State	admitted June 20, 1863
Tree	Sugar Maple
Flower	Rhododendron
Bird	Cardinal

WHILE IN WEST VIRGINIA...

CAMP — in State Parks, many with playgrounds and game courts; others feature tennis, golf, horseback riding, hiking, a seasonal naturalist.

MARVEL — at glassware artisans — glass blowers and hand decorators; or at craftsmen demonstrating traditional skills — from candle making and quilting to weaving.

WALK — Harpers Ferry, the old town associated with abolitionist John Brown, or step further back in time into a 1776 Revolutionary War fort.

TRAVEL — in a coal car through underground passageways of a coal mine with a former miner as guide.

TOUR — a living pioneer farm with 21 reconstructed buildings, or visit gristmills, some have been grinding grain into flour since the 1800's.

OVERLOOK — three states at Prospect Peak, listen to the music from limestone pipes in Organ Cave, or drive through a twin-barrelled covered bridge.

FISH — in rivers, reservoirs and lakes for four varieties of trout, bass, walleye, and more.

SKI — on snow or grass in Canann Valley, or Snowshoe with a 1500-foot drop.

★ ★ ★ ★ ★ ★

WRITE — for more information: Division of Tourism and Parks, State Capitol, Charleston, WV 25305. 1-800-CALL-WVA.

TRY...

HAM SLICES IN FRUIT JUICE
or
BATTER FRIED CHICKEN
or
BRUNSWICK STEW, *see Virginia*
serve with
ALMOST BAKED POTATOES, *see Washington*
BUTTERED BROCCOLI
BLACKBERRY FLUMMERY

An old West Virginia recipe starts with uncooked ham, soaked overnight, then boiled with lemons, oranges, apricots, prunes and cloves; finally covered with brown sugar, studded with cloves and baked. You can achieve a similar flavor with:

HAM SLICES IN FRUIT JUICE

Pre-cooked ham slices, about ½ inch thick   Fruit juices

Pour enough fruit juice in skillet to cover the bottom. (You can use the liquid from any canned fruit, adding some lemon and orange juice if desired.) Place ham slices in pan, stick in a few cloves, then barely cover ham with more juice. Simmer slowly, covered, for about 20 minutes. Remove ham, keep warm, then rapidly boil juice to thicken — or if you're in a hurry, stir in about a tablespoon of cornstarch mixed with 2 tablespoons of water and cook until thick.

"Blackberrying" is an old West Virginia custom. It was usually an all-day affair and the picnic lunch inevitably included fried chicken, usually cut in small pieces before serving. It was said locally to replace bread as the staff of life.

BATTER FRIED CHICKEN

2-3 lbs. drumsticks and thighs   1 egg
1 c biscuit or pancake mix   ⅔ c milk

Measure mix into medium bowl. Beat egg with fork, add milk. Stir into mix. Heat shortening or oil in large pan (about ¼ inch deep). Dip chicken pieces into batter, allowing excess to drip off. Fry until crisp and brown (about 20 minutes), turning as needed. 4 to 6 servings.

The results from blackberry picking were made into cobblers, pies, jams, preserves, or juiced and made into old-fashioned:

BLACKBERRY FLUMMERY

¾ c sugar   2 c blackberry juice*
3 T cornstarch   2 T lemon juice

Mix sugar and cornstarch in a saucepan. Gradually stir in blackberry juice and lemon juice. Cook over medium heat, stirring constantly, until boiling. Boil one minute. Chill. Serve with cream or whipped topping.

*Note: It takes about 1½ quarts berries to make two cups of juice. Mash berries, simmer, then strain. A cloth-covered metal strainer lets you push the berries to extract the juice, and keeps the seeds from escaping.

WISCONSIN — THE BADGER STATE

Capital	Madison
Elevation	581 ft to 1953 ft.
Population (1980)	4,765,000
(1990)	4,816,000
30th State	admitted May 29, 1848
Tree	Sugar Maple
Flower	Wood Violet
Bird	Robin

WHILE IN WISCONSIN...

CAMP   in your choice of varying sites from Lake Michigan's beaches or rocky shoreline to scenic river areas with canyons and waterfalls.

TOUR   a cheese factory, fish hatchery, a paper mill, a barrel factory; or one of the breweries that "made Milwaukee famous."

ENJOY   an ice cream sundae at Two Rivers, point of origin and sold only on Sundays. Then troll Lake Michigan in a charter boat.

SEE   to believe a 16-foot Loon statue; "Chatty Belle", a talking cow statue; and a 4-story high "Musky" with an observation deck inside its jaws.

PLAY   a word game with the kids, each listing as many Indian and French-sounding geographical names within the state as you can.

BROWSE   through "America's Little Switzerland", settled by Swiss immigrants in 1845, a replica of a pioneer village, specializing in Swiss delicacies.

YOU'LL   "get it all" at Old World Wisconsin where 40 authentic, original structures represent the state's many ethnic cultures. Costumed guides at each.

★ ★ ★ ★ ★ ★ ★

WRITE   for more information: Wisconsin Tourism Development, P.O. Box 7970, Madison, WI 53702. Or call: 1-800-432-TRIP.

TRY

CORNISH PASTIES, SIMPLIFIED
or
CAMPERS' ROAST
with CAMPFIRE POTATOES, *see Colorado*
or
SWEDISH MEATBALLS, *see Minnesota*
with noodles
serve with
HOT GREEN BEAN SALAD, *see Rhode Island*
APPLE PIE from a bakery and Wisconsin cheese

Cornishmen who came to Wisconsin to work in the lead and zinc mines, introduced pasties to the United States. These were carried for lunch, and reheated over the candle worn on the miners' hats.

CORNISH PASTIES, SIMPLIFIED

½ lb. round steak
1 or 2 med. raw potatoes
1 small raw turnip
½ c onion, chopped
½ t salt
¼ t pepper
2 (8 oz.) cans refrigerated crescent rolls

Cut beef, the peeled potatoes and turnips into ¼-inch cubes. Stir vegetables, meat and seasonings together, blending well.
meat and seasonings together, blending well.

Unroll the crescent rolls (two at a time), and on lightly floured board, place two triangles together to make a rectangle, overlapping the joined edges slightly. Roll dough into 8-inch squares. Turn each square so a point faces you. (Now looks like a diamond.)

Place about ½ cup of meat and vegetable mixture on half of the diamond nearest you; spreading filling to within ½-inch of the edges. Fold over the top half, then seal the pastry edges by pressing with tines of a fork. Cut several slits on top to let steam escape. Place on an ungreased baking sheet and bake in a 400° oven about 30 minutes until brown. 8 pasties.

With the westward expansion after the Civil War, lumber for houses was much in demand. To fill the need, timber-cutters swarmed into the forests of Wisconsin, Minnesota and Michigan which became known as the Lumberjack Frontier. Roasted meat was a favorite, and the tradition continues.

LUMBERJACK ROAST

1 (3-4 lb.) boneless roast, about 2 inches thick
¼ c soy sauce
¼ c lemon juice
¼ c oil
1 stalk celery
include leaves
1 med. onion, sliced
pepper to taste

Make a pan (to loosely fit the roast) of heavy duty aluminum foil, by turning up the sides and folding the corners. Place the "pan" on a large rectangular piece of foil -- large enough to make a butcher seal over the top, lengthwise, and to seal the ends tightly.

Put in the roast, sprinkle with pepper, and pour over liquid ingredients. Place celery stalk* and onion* on the meat. Now seal as directed above.

★ Alice Peters, Kimberly, WI

WYOMING — THE EQUALITY STATE

Capital	Cheyenne
Elevation	3100 ft to. 13,804 ft.
Population (1980)	502,000
(1990)	507,000
44th State	admitted July 10, 1890
Tree	Cottonwood
Flower	Indian Paintbrush
Bird	Meadowlark

WHILE IN WYOMING...

CAMP in the majestic Grand Tetons, or near the geysers of Yellowstone National Park, or by Devil's Tower.

FOLLOW the Oregon Trail, "The First Road West", and discover historic sites, wagon ruts, trading posts and Pony Express stations.

FISH for trout and 21 other species of game fish in mountain streams, slow-moving rivers or catch brown trout in Flaming Gorge Lake.

EXPLORE State Parks, including the Buffalo Bill Historical Center, Hot Springs, Sinks Canyon where a river disappears, and Seminoe with its white sand dunes.

CHEER the rodeo stars, watch parades, admire Indian dancers, and join the festivities at Cheyenne Frontier Days, the world's biggest outdoor rodeo.

WATCH antelopes race near highways, or visit numerous National Forests teeming with wildlife, from the yellow bellied marmot to the majestic elk.

SKI in any of 56 resorts, including Teton Village with a vertical rise of 4,139 feet; or travel a snowmobile trail.

★ ★ ★ ★ ★ ★

WRITE for more information: Division of Tourism, Frank Norris, Jr. Travel Center, Cheyenne, WY 82002.

TRY

GRILLED LAMB CHOPS
or
CALICO BEANS
or
DORIS' SURPRISE PACKAGE, *see Nevada*
serve with
CARROT AND RAISIN SALAD, *see Utah*
WHOLE WHEAT FRENCH BREAD
FRONTIER POPCORN

Lamb chops grilled over an open fire was a frequent meal of the Basque shepherds, called from their mountain homes between Spain and France to tend sheep in many parts of the American Northwest.

GRILLED LAMB CHOPS

Lamb chops, ½ to ¾ inch thick
Canned pears, mint jelly for garnish

Slash into the edges of fat around the chops. Lightly grease grate, and place chops over hot coals. Grill 8 to 10 minutes, then turn and cook another 5 to 8 minutes until done to your taste. For oven broiling, place chops about 3 or 4 inches from heat, allowing the same amount of time. For pan broiling, heat griddle first, sprinkle in a little salt, put in chops and continue as for grilling.

An old cook book lists an incredible number of recipes for Wyoming dried beans, including Bean Bread, Cookies and Fudge, but we'll settle for:

CALICO BEANS

1 (16 oz.) can **each** lima beans, kidney beans, pork and beans
½ lb. bacon
1 c onion, chopped
½ c catsup
1 T prepared mustard
¾ c brown sugar
1 T vinegar

Drain lima beans; drain kidney beans, reserving liquid for later use. Fry bacon until crisp, crumble and set aside. Pour off all but 2 tablespoons fat and brown onion in same skillet. Mix in the rest of the ingredients, including bacon, and simmer, covered, for 15 minutes. Uncover and continue cooking over low heat for another 15 minutes. If the mixture seems too thick, stir in part or all of reserve liquid from the kidney beans.

★ Arlene Sears, Jackson, CA

Early frontiersmen sweetened their popcorn by making a syrup in a heavy kettle over a wood fire. Use a large, deep kettle for best results.

FRONTIER POPCORN

Combine 1 tablespoon butter or margarine, 3 tablespoons water and ¾ cup sugar in large saucepan. Boil until hard ball stage. Mix in 3 quarts of popped corn and stir until kernels are well coated.

BREAKFASTS

When you're in the mood for eggs, try these.

BASTED EGGS

After cooking bacon until crispness desired; set aside to drain on paper towels. Pour off all but 2 or 3 tablespoons bacon grease. Break eggs carefully into hot fat. Cook slowly, dipping fat over top of yolks after white begins to set. Cook until white is firm. Serve on toast.

COUNTRY FRIED EGGS

Lightly grease frying pan; break in eggs. Add a tablespoon of water per egg and cover. Cook slowly. These are halfway between fried and poached eggs. Super on toasted English muffins.

SCRAMBLED EGG VARIATIONS

Stir in several drops of Worcestershire sauce per egg before scrambling.

OR: add 2 tablespoons cottage cheese per egg when eggs are nearly done.

OR: for four eggs, stir in ½ cup grated cheddar cheese.

OR: add a small can of drained mushrooms (use liquid from mushrooms instead of milk or water when fork-whipping eggs.)

OR: stretch with 3 or 4 crumbled soda crackers, chopped wieners, ham or bologna.

BREAKFAST SANDWICH

Per person — 1 English muffin, slice of ham or Canadian bacon, 1 slice American cheese, 1 egg. Toast muffin, warm meat, cook egg to your taste. Assemble by placing meat on muffin, top with egg, cheese and other muffin half.

GILDED EGGS

1 (10½ oz.) can Cheddar   6 hard-cooked eggs,
    cheese soup   sliced
⅓ c milk   6 slices toast

In a medium saucepan, heat soup and milk, stirring contantly. Stir in egg slices gently; heat through. Spoon over toast. Garnish with snipped chives or green onions, and bacon bits, if desired.

ZUCCHINI FRITATTA

see Washington

A favorite Girl Scout trick is:
SKILLET DOUGHNUTS
Use canned refrigerator biscuits (any variety). Separate biscuits. Put thumbs in the middle of each biscuit to make a hole. Stretch a little and turn inside out to make a ring. Fry in ¼-inch fat in frying pan. Sprinkle with cinnamon sugar.

A different way to use canned biscuits is in:
SUNSHINE CIRCLES
Peel and separate an orange into segments. Flatten canned biscuits into about 3-inch circles (until ¼-inch thick). Place a segment or two (depending on size of orange) on one biscuit, top with another and pinch edges to seal. Bake as directed.

OR:

When you have some nice, hot coals for a breakfast fire, use canned biscuits for:
BUTTERY BITES
1 tube refrigerator biscuits   Butter or margarine, melted

Cut each biscuit into fourths, then thread on a long skewer or opened-up wire clothes hanger. Leave about ½ inch between each piece of dough. Hold over hot coals until puffed and brown. Dunk into melted butter or maragarine.

Surprise your family with this:
QUICK ORANGE COFFEECAKE
12 brown and serve rolls
or 1 (10 oz.) can refrigerator biscuits
2 T sugar
2 T frozen orange juice concentrate, undiluted
1 T butter or margarine
½ c flaked coconut

Put rolls or biscuits in baking pan. Gently pierce each two or three times with large-tined cooking fork.

Combine sugar, concentrate, and butter in small saucepan and heat slowly until sugar dissolves, stirring constantly. Add cocnut, then spread mixture over rolls. Bake in preheated oven according to package directions — about 8 or 10 minutes.

★ C. Bedard, Wewahitchka, FL

Special Breakfasts

Use up leftover potatoes in:
YELLOWJACKETS FOR BREAKFAST

5 slices bacon, cut in 1" pieces	3 or 4 cooked potatoes, diced
1 med. onion, chopped	salt and pepper
4 eggs, slightly beaten	

Fry bacon in heavy skillet. Remove when brown. Drain off fat, leaving 2 tablespoons in pan. Add onions and cook slowly until golden. (The onions may be omitted and no harm done.) Stir in potatoes, salt and pepper. Cook 5 minutes. Pour eggs over potatoes, break yolks, but wait until whites are beginning to set before stirring. This keeps the good bright yellow of the yolks. Cook until eggs are done, but not dry. Top with crumbled bacon. 4 servings.

Want an "only one plate to wash" breakfast? Try this:
SAUSAGE AND APPLE BUNS

1 lb. brown & serve sausages	2 T sugar
2 apples, peeled and sliced	dash of salt
	6 hamburger buns

Brown sausage. Add sliced apples. Sprinkle with sugar and salt. Cover and cook on medium until apples are tender (7-8 minutes.)

Split and toast buns. Place on large plate. Let all "eaters" help themselves.

If you have been a lucky fisherman, or the camper next to you has been super lucky, you may enjoy this:

SPECIAL TROUT BREAKFAST

individual cans of fruit juice	sauteed trout
fried potatoes	coffee or milk

Peel one potato for each person. Cut in four lengthwise and slice thinly into ¼ cup oil or bacon fat in hot skillet. Add salt and pepper and ½ cup water. Cover and cook 5-7 minutes. Turn potatoes and cover; cook another 5-6 minutes until done.

Meanwhile, heat ½ cup oil or bacon fat in heavy frying pan. Season ½ cup cornmeal with salt and pepper. Roll trout in this mixture. Cook in hot fat about 4 minutes on each side until well browned.

PANCAKE POSSIBILITIES

Start with your favorite pancake mix and go from there.

CORN PANCAKES

Stir in 1 (8 oz.) can whole kernel corn, drained.

CORNMEAL CAKES

Reduce pancake mix from 2 cups to 1½ cups, add 2 tablespoons oil, ½ cup cornmeal.

OR: for a different taste, use ¼ cup wheat germ, or uncooked wheat cereal (such as Wheat Heart, Malt-O-Meal, etc.)

CHEESE PANCAKES

Keep regular 2-cup proportions, then stir in ½-1 cup grated cheddar cheese.

FRUIT PANCAKES

For "shortcake" type, simply add 1 or 2 tablespoons sugar to regular recipe, cook as usual, then top warm cakes with fresh berries or fresh or canned peaches and top with whipped cream or whipped topping.

For FRUITED PANCAKES, add to batter ½-1 cup canned or fresh blueberries.

OR: 1 (8 oz.) can crushed pineapple, drained.

OR: 1 chopped apple and ½ teaspoon each of nutmeg and cinnamon. Cook as usual.

Bonus Hint: If you have batter left over, fry in large cakes and save for lunch to wrap around wieners or top with hot chili.

MISCELLANEOUS

Pennsylvania has an interesting breakfast dish which the residents call "PANHAUS", but we know as SCRAPPLE. It is made by cooking bits of pork with cornmeal until thick, poured into a pan to cool, then turned out and sliced, dipped in flour and browned in hot fat. It is traditionally served with a tart fruit sauce. Fortunately it is sold by the can, and is easy to slice if you cut off both ends of the can reserving one to push out the scrapple.

Here's a real old-timer:

GOLDEN BARS

When you cook any of the wheat cereals, make a double batch. Pour the unused portion into a small bread pan; chill overnight. In the morning, slice about ½ inch thick and fry in fat (preferrably bacon) until golden brown. Serve with butter and maple syrup. Just don't call it "fried mush"!

LUNCHES — Cold Sandwiches

Do you know that sandwiches were named for John Montagu, 4th Earl of Sandwich way back in the middle of the 18th century? Maybe you do know that your hungry family eats lots of them.

HELP-YOURSELF-SANDWICHES

Start with a loaf of bread, some butter, and a jar of mayonnaise. Set to one side a jar of peanut butter and a jar of jelly or jam or some raisins. On a tray arrange any cold sliced meat or sausage, add slices of cheese, pickles, catsup, chili sauce, mustard and a dish of relish for garnishing. Carrot and celery sticks help fill the vacant spots. Pass the milk or fruit punch and with cookies or fresh fruit, they will all say they had a good lunch.

A different kind of sandwich from the usual egg-salad variety is:
SLICED EGG SANDWICH
6 hard-cooked eggs   salt and pepper
mayonnaise

Spread 12 slices of bread with mayonnaise. Slice eggs lengthwise (1 to each sandwich) sprinkle with salt and pepper. That's an egg sandwich.

OR:
"SUPER" EGG SANDWICHES

To the above recipe add 1 (4 oz.) can of green chilis. Remove any seeds from the chilis and carefully spread them over the sliced eggs before putting on the top slice of bread. May add a lettuce leaf or shredded lettuce if you wish.

Bonus Hint: Don't waste time and effort hard-cooking 6 eggs. Simmer a dozen (mark cooked eggs with an X) and store on ice or in the refrigerator. They keep well.

You can use two of those pre-cooked eggs in:
TUNA SALAD SANDWICH

Chop and mix together: 1 can tuna, 2 hard-cooked eggs, 2 T pickles of your choice and 2 T onions. Add mayonnaise to moisten.

DEVILED WIENER SANDWICH

Grind or grate 1 lb. wieners and enough carrots to make 2 cups. Stir in 1 tablespoon prepared mustard and ¼ cup sweet pickle relish. Add enough mayonnaise or salad dressing to make a nice spreading consistency.

Hot Sandwiches

Hot sandwiches are filling for lunch, or good for the evening meal with a mug of hot tomato soup; served with carrot sticks, radishes, sliced cucumber or zucchini or pickles of your choice. Run a whizzer on your family or friends, serve steaming mugs of hot chocolate and tell them that is "Dessert in a Mug". Maybe you'll get by with it.

CHILI DOGS

8 wieners	8 warmed hotdog buns
1 (1 lb.) can chili	1 small onion, chopped

Split hot dogs lengthwise and brown lightly in oil in hot pan. Push aside and brown onions. Add chili and cook until well heated.

Place hot dog in bun and spoon chili mixture over it. It's wise to put all this on a plate and pass the forks.

Wieners are also good in:
BOSTON BEAN SANDWICH

1 lrg. onion, chopped	1 (16 oz.) can baked beans
oil or butter	½ c pickle relish
1 lb. wieners	½ c catsup

Cook onion in oil or butter. Cut wieners in small slices. Add remaining ingredients and bring to a boil. Allow to simmer about 5 minutes. Serve over heated or toasted hamburger buns. 4 to 6 servings.

OR in:
HOT DOG STEW

1 lb. wieners	2 (16 oz.) cans tomatoes

Heat sliced wieners with tomatoes; simmer until thickened. Serve over noodles, rice or split hamburger buns.

Vegetable soup adds a new taste to:
JOE'S SUPER FAST SLOPPIES

Brown ½ pound ground beef. Drain off fat. Add 1 (10½ oz.) can undiluted vegetable soup. Heat through. Serve on hamburger buns with carrot, cucumber or zucchini sticks.

★ Ronda Wisniewski, S. Plainfield, NJ

CHEESY BEANIE BUNS

1 can pork and beans	warm buttered buns
3 T chili sauce or catsup	shredded cheese or
2 T sweet pickle relish	cheese slices

Combine beans, catsup and relish and heat through. Spread mixture on buns and top with shredded cheese.

POCKETBOOK SANDWICHES

4 thin slices ham
4 slices cheese
2 T oil for fryin
4 buns or Pita pockets
(warmed) dill pickles
or prepared mustard

Fold ham around cheese slice, fasten with a toothpick. Brown these "pocketbooks" on both sides in hot oil until cheese begins to melt. Slip into buns or Pita pockets with dill pickle slices, relish, and/or mustard.

BARBECUED LUNCHEON MEAT ON A BUN

Cut luncheon meat in thick slices. Grill slices brushing frequently with barbecue sauce. Serve on toasted buns with slices of tomato and onion.

CHILI BUNS

1 lb. ground beef
1 sm. onion, chopped
1 (15 oz.) can chili with beans
1 (8 oz.) can tomato sauce
½ c chili sauce (hot)
¼ green pepper, chopped, optional
8 hamburger buns

In a large frying pan, lightly brown beef, onion and pepper. Pour off excess fat. Add chili, soups, chili sauce. Heat through. Spread on buns. 8 servings.

SKILLET HAM & CHEESE

4 slices ham (luncheon meat or bologna)
4 slices cheese
8 slices bread
3 T oil

Form 4 sandwiches. Saute in oil in a large skillet. Turn once during cooking. Ready to eat when slightly brown and cheese is melting. Serve with pickles, relish, mustard or carrot sticks. 4 servings.

CORNED BEEF SANDWICHES

1 (1 lb.) can corned beef hash
¼ c chopped onion
¼ c sweet pickle relish
2 T oil
bread or buns
for 8 servings.

Combine hash, onion and pickle relish. Place in frying pan with oil. Heat thoroughly. Toast bread or buns.

Spread hot hash on bread or buns. Serve immediately with carrot, celery, cucumber or zucchini slices. Dill pickles are very good with these sandwiches.

Special Lunches

Quick-cooking oriental noodles, Ramen, can give you a change of pace for lunch. Serve them plain with crackers and cheese, or sturdy them up in:

HEAP SOUP

To the two cups of water per package you're boiling for the noodles, add any pleasing combination of leftover cooked meat or fish and vegetables. When the water begins to boil, add the noodles and proceed as usual.

OR: you can use fresh vegetables such as celery, onions, carrots, bell peppers, cauliflower, broccoli, snow peas. Cook until almost as tender as you prefer, then add the noodles and seasoning packet.

Another satisfying, quickly made hot lunch is:

ZUCCHINI FRITTERS

3 c grated zucchini	1 c biscuit mix
1 egg, slightly beaten	oil for frying
½ t salt	parmesan cheese

Mix above ingredients, except parmesan cheese which is sprinkled on top at serving time. Drop by large spoonfuls on a hot griddle. Turn when underside is brown. 4 servings.

OR:

ZUCCHINI SCRAMBLE

Crumble ½ pound hamburger and brown in skillet. Add some chopped onion and zucchini, sliced thin. Brown all together, then stir in 2 or 3 eggs, and cook until eggs are done.

An old-fashioned treat is:

CORNED BEEF HASH AND EGGS

Spread one (16 oz.) can of corned beef hash in a frying pan. Make 4 indentations about 2 inches in diameter. Place over low heat and break one egg into each depression. Salt and pepper the eggs. Cover and cook until eggs are done. Cut in wedges or squares (depending on the shape of your skillet), and serve with toast.

CAMPER'S FRUIT SALAD

Into Cottage Cheese, stir fresh berries, any fruit cut in small cubes, also melon cuts, or any combination of berries, fruits or melons. Drained canned fruit cocktail may be used. The salad will be more hearty if salted peanuts are sprinkled on top. Serve on crisp lettuce.

BEVERAGES

Make this at home to take along in a quart jar.
HOT CHOCOLATE MIX
3 c nonfat dry milk   ¾ c cocoa
1 c sugar   1 T salt

Mix dry milk and sugar. Add cocoa and salt and stir until thoroughly mixed. Store in covered container. To serve: stir two heaping tablespoons dry mix into an 9 ounce cup or glass with hot or cold water. Makes 32 eight ounce servings.

Another refreshing hot or cold beverage mix is:
CAMPFIRE TEA
½ c instant tea   1 c sugar
½ c dry orange drink   Dash of ground cloves,
½ c dry lemonade mix   optional

Mix all ingredients together thoroughly. Put 2 or more teaspoonsful (to taste) in a cup of hot water; or mix in a glass with cold wate and ice. Keep in a covered container. Makes about 60 eight ounce servings.

If you have some chocolate syrup on hand try:
MOCHA COFFEE
For each serving, pour one tablespoon chocolate syrup in a mug. Fill with hot coffee and stir to blend.

If you run out of milk, coffee cream or powdered creamer; and you're lucky enough to have some canned whipped cream, whipped topping or even powdered whip — spray a dab of the former, or stir in the others to make a SPECIAL COFFEE.

★ *Cathy Nign, Temple City, CA*

Bouillon needn't be just a soup dish. Stir a teaspoon of granules, or a bouillon cube for a hot change-of-pace drink to cut the evening's chill.

Our favorite hot weather drink, or by adding an egg, a quick breakfast treat is:
ORANGE AUGUSTUS
1 can (6 oz.) frozen orange juice concentrate (undiluted)
1 c EACH milk and water   1 t vanilla
⅓ to ¼ c sugar   8 ice cubes
                         (about 1 cup)

Combine all ingredients in a blender, and run at medium-high speed until you can no longer hear the ice rattling. (Toss in an egg or two, and you've added protein.) Serves 4.

★ *Karen Richards, Snohomish, WA*

RECIPE INDEX

BEVERAGES 116

BREADS
Chuckwagon Biscuits, 79
Hush Puppies, 91
Johnnycakes, 55

BREAKFASTS 108 — 111

DESSERTS
Banana Sandwich, 87
Blackberry Flummery, 103
Blueberry Slump, 65
Blueberry Pie, 19
Brown Bears in the Apple Orchard, 35
Frontier Popcorn, 107
Cherry Crisp, 51
Coffee Can Ice Cream, 57
Covered Wagon Candy, 95
Dippin' Strawberries, 9
Fresh Berry "Shortcakes", 53
Gateway Gingerbread, 59
Grapes with Sour Cream, 71
Honey Popcorn Squares, 37
Key Lime Pie, 25
Maple Syrup Treat, 97
Melon Fruit Cup, 47
Orange Ambrosia, 41
Peppermint Orange, 4
Patriotic Pudding, 23
Rocky Road Cookies, 63
Sheer Bliss, 11
Shoofly Pie, 83
South Fulton Banana Pudding, 91
Spicy Applesauce, 77
Summer Pudding, 81
Swamp Huckleberry Pudding, 67
Texas Ambrosia, 93

LUNCHES 112 — 115

MAIN DISHES
BEANS
Calico Beans, 107
Campers' Baked Beans and Brown Bread, 49
Chili-Mac, 95
Dorothy's Texas Chili, 93
Great Lakes Dip or Dinner, 51
Pasta E Fagioli, 71
Spanish Beans, 79

Taco Salad, 15

CHICKEN
Arroz Con Pollo, 11
Batter Fried Chicken, 103
Braised Chicken, 85
Brunswick Stew, 99
Campers' Burgoo, 41
Campers' Jambalaya, 43
Chicken Corn Soup, 83
Chicken 'N Noodles, 39
Chicken Gabriella, 101
Chicken Paprika, 93
Chicken with Southern Barbecue Sauce, 7
Chicken Teriyaki, 29
Country Captain Chicken, 27
Easy Southern-Fried Chicken, 73
Grand Strand Chicken Bog, 87
Grilled Lemon Chicken, 17
Maryland Chicken, 47
Simple Chicken Fricassee, 75
Skillet Chicken with Dumplings, 89
Sue's "Souper" Fast Chicken Pot Pie, 89

FISH & SEAFOOD
Aunt Jenny's Catfish, 55
Baltimore Crab Louis, 47
Bass and Bananas, 53
Bass Fillets, 41
Campers' Clam Spaghetti, 67
Cape Cod Clam Chowder, 49
Catfish Stew, 87
Connecticut Brook Trout, 19
Crab Patties, 27
Crispy Fried Fish, 7
Delaware Crab Cakes, 21
Easy Salmon Spread, 9
Fisherman's Stew, 57
Kedgeree, 85
Kitchen Stove Clambake, 81
Maine Lobster Stew, 45
Manhattan Clam Chowder, 71
Marinated Salmon Steaks, 9
New Orleans Creole Gumbo, 43
Pan Fried Cat Fish, 91
Pan Fried Scrod, 65
Sauteed Pompano, 93
Shrimp Egg Foo Yung, 29
Shrimp Gumbo, 55
Steamed Clams, 21
Whole Trout Cooked in Foil, 17

MEATS
Braised Venison Loin Chops, 31
Campers' Delight, 77
Campers' Delight with Polish
 Sausage, 51
Campers' Jambalaya, 43
Campfire Steak, 79
Chop Suey Burgers, 15
Chuckwagon Skillet, 39
Cider-Braised Ham, 73
Cincinnati Pork Chops, 77
Colonial Hashed Beef on Buns, 97
Corned Beef and Cabbage, 65
Cornish Pasties, Simplified, 105
Denver Sandwich, 17
Doris' Surprise Package, 9
Fried Ham with Red-Eye Gravy, 99
Grilled Bratwurst, 89
Grilled Lamb Chops, 107
Grilled Reuben, 61
Ham Slices in Fruit Juice, 103
Hominy Harmony, 61
Honolulu Pork and Pineapple, 29
Horseradish Steak, 33
Hot Dog Goulash, 13
Hot Dogs in a Corn Blanket, 23
Lumberjack Roast, 105
Luncheon Meat Barbecue, 37
Maple Spareribs, 35
Mormon Split Pea Soup, 95
Orange Sauced Ham Steaks, 25
Pan Barbecued Spareribs, 11
Pan Broiled Buffalo Steaks, 59
Porcupine Meat Balls, Quick, 63
Pork Chops with Stuffing, 31
Pork Pot Pie, 83
Posole, 69
Red Flannel Hash, 19
Sausage with Hominy, 35
Senate Bean Soup, 23
Stacked Enchiladas, 69
Swedish Meatballs, 53
Swiss Hero Sandwich, 33
Taco Salad, 15
Tangy Pork Chops, 13
Wiener Schnitzel, 37
Wieners and Sauerkraut, 75

PASTA, POTATOES, RICE
Almost Baked Potatoes, 101
Campfire Potatoes, 17
Hopping John, 87
Platter Macaroni, 75
Sheepherder's Potatoes, 63
Skillet Scalloped Potatoes, 97
Spanish Settler's Rice, 69

SALADS
All American Potato Salad, 33
Calico Potato Salad, 53
Carrot and Raisin Salad, 95
Cole Slaw, Southern Style, 7
Cool-Down Salad, 11
Fresh Spinach Salad, 43
Green and Gold Salad, 15
Green Bean and Onion Salad, 21
Hot Green Bean Salad, 85
Hot Potato Salad, 89
Monster Salad, 67
Pineapple Cole Slaw, 99
Potato-Shrimp Salad, 24
Sunshine Salad, 59
Taco Salad, 15
Yankee Slaw, 49

VEGETABLES
Barbecued Corn in the Husks, 61
Corn Oysters, 45
Foil Baked Veggies, 5
Fresh Sprouts, 5
Hot Cabbage Slaw, 39
Hot Green Beans, 13
Stir-fry Vegetables, Chinese Style, 15
Succotash, 67
Vegetable Medley, 81
Zucchini Fritatta, 101

MISCELLANEOUS
Campsite Popcorn, 4
Cream Gravy, 73
Gwen's Cream Soup Mix, 4
Jerky, 4
Easy Salmon Spread, 9
Quick Chinese Sauce, 29
Tangy Bacon Dressing, 43

WANT MORE GREAT COOKING??? SURE!

"All American Cooking: Savory Recipes from Savvy, Creative Cooks Across America" by Meryl Nelson. Here are some of the best historical and regional recipes from across America. You'll love it! Also includes "Things to see and do in every state." A Great Gift Idea! Price $9.95. Order Number 902.

"This For That: A Treasury of Savvy Substitutions for the Creative Cook" by Meryl Nelson. Meryl's cookbooks are nationally famous. *This For That* has been featured in Family Circle and many other national publications, TV and radio. Hints, Recipes, How-To's for using THIS when you're out of THAT, includes microwave directions. Price $6.95. Order Number 847.

"The Newlywed Cookbook" by Robin Walsh. Bet you have a wedding to go to soon—here is the perfect wedding gift to add to a set of hand towels or an appliance. *The Newlywed Cookbook* is the perfect kitchen gift along with our other titles listed here. The Famous *Chef Tell* says, "Amusing, creative ideas for the beginner cook. I highly recommend it!" Price $12.95. Order Number 877.

Kids Love To Cook. So how about teaching them with "Learning Through Cooking: A Cooking Program for Children Two to Ten" by Nancy Ferreira. They will learn many important things with this GREAT little book. Price $7.95. Order Number 658.

The Lowfat Mexican Cookbook: True Mexican Taste Without the WAIST by Robert and Nancy Leos. If you love Mexican foods as much as we do, but do not want the extra calories it contains, than this is just what the chef needs. Good eating as well as good health are here in this great little book. Price $6.95. Order Number 896.

YOUR ORDER

ORDER #	QTY	UNIT PRICE	TOTAL PRICE

Please rush me the following books. I want to save by ordering three books and receive FREE shipping charges. Orders under 3 books please include $2.50 shipping. CA residents add 8.25% tax.

SHIP TO:

(Please Print) Name: _____
Organization: _____
Address: _____
City/State/Zip: _____

PAYMENT METHOD

☐ Enclosed check or money order

☐ MasterCard   Card Expires _____   Signature _____

☐ Visa

R & E Publishers • P.O. Box 2008 • Saratoga, CA 95070 (408) 866-6303 FAX (408) 866-1825

WANT MORE GREAT COOKING??? SURE!

"All American Cooking: Savory Recipes from Savvy, Creative Cooks Across America" by Meryl Nelson. Here are some of the best historical and regional recipes from across America. You'll love it! Also includes "Things to see and do in every state." A Great Gift Idea! Price $9.95. Order Number 902.

"This For That: A Treasury of Savvy Substitutions for the Creative Cook" by Meryl Nelson. Meryl's cookbooks are nationally famous. *This For That* has been featured in Family Circle and many other national publications, TV and radio. Hints, Recipes, How-To's for using THIS when you're out of THAT, includes microwave directions. Price $6.95. Order Number 847.

"The Newlywed Cookbook" by Robin Walsh. Bet you have a wedding to go to soon—here is the perfect wedding gift to add to a set of hand towels or an appliance. *The Newlywed Cookbook* is the perfect kitchen gift along with our other titles listed here. The Famous *Chef Tell* says, "Amusing, creative ideas for the beginner cook. I highly recommend it!" Price $12.95. Order Number 877.

Kids Love To Cook. So how about teaching them with "Learning Through Cooking: A Cooking Program for Children Two to Ten" by Nancy Ferreira. They will learn many important things with this GREAT little book. Price $7.95. Order Number 658.

The Lowfat Mexican Cookbook: True Mexican Taste Without the WAIST by Robert and Nancy Leos. If you love Mexican foods as much as we do, but do not want the extra calories it contains, than this is just what the chef needs. Good eating as well as good health are here in this great little book. Price $6.95. Order Number 896.

YOUR ORDER

ORDER #	QTY	UNIT PRICE	TOTAL PRICE

Please rush me the following books. I want to save by ordering three books and receive FREE shipping charges. Orders under 3 books please include $2.50 shipping. CA residents add 8.25% tax.

SHIP TO:

(Please Print) Name: _____

Organization: _____

Address: _____

City/State/Zip: _____

PAYMENT METHOD

☐ Enclosed check or money order

☐ MasterCard   Card Expires _____   Signature _____

☐ Visa | | | | | | | | | | | | | |

R & E Publishers • P.O. Box 2008 • Saratoga, CA 95070 (408) 866-6303 FAX (408) 866-1825